JAPANESE-STYLE MANAGEMENT TRANSFERRED:
THE EXPERIENCE OF EAST ASIA

JAPANESE-STYLE MANAGEMENT TRANSFERRED
The Experience of East Asia

K. John Fukuda

ROUTLEDGE
London and New York

First published in 1988 by
Routledge
11 New Fetter Lane, London EC4P 4EE
29 West 35th Street, New York, NY 10001

© 1988 K. John Fukuda

Printed in Great Britain by
Billing & Sons Ltd, Worcester

British Library Cataloguing in Publication Data

Fukuda, K.J.
    Japanese style management transferred:
    the experience of East Asia.
    1. East Asia. Industries. Management
    I. Title
    658'.00951
    ISBN 0-415-01266-X

To My Father and Mother

CONTENTS

List of Figures
List of Tables
Foreword and Acknowledgements

CONTENTS

Appendix   CHINESE MANAGEMENT:
           WHATEVER HAPPENED TO ITS TRADITIONS?

LIST OF FIGURES

LIST OF TABLES

Japan's phenomenal rise to economic superpower during the post-war period may be explained by many factors. However, it is now generally agreed that the country's economic miracle is largely attributable to its unique style of management as practiced in the home country. In recent years, Japan's direct investment overseas has begun to grow at an accelerating pace, in large part, due to the drastic appreciation of Japanese yen since 1985. As a result, the home-grown practices of Japanese-style management are also being exported abroad by an increasing number of Japanese companies setting up or expanding their overseas operations.

While numerous studies have been carried out to determine the transferability of Japanese-style management to developed countries in the West, very few have examined this issue with a specific focus on East Asia. As the economy of the region expands faster than elsewhere, Japan is increasingly expected, and has indeed accepted, to play a more active role as the leader of neighboring countries. In fact, Asia's four newly industrialized countries - South Korea, Taiwan, Hong Kong and Singapore - have themselves achieved the economic mini-miracle during the first half of the 1980s. Today these four countries, often labeled as the "Four Small Dragons", are following the footpath taken not so long ago by Japan - the "Big Dragon".

This book, based on extensive original research, examines both the problems and opportunities involved with the transfer of Japanese-style management practices to other areas in East Asia. With an aim to fill the gap left by other studies conducted mostly in the Western context, the study attempts to move forward the comparative management theory on the basis of data collected from East Asian, rather than Euro-American, cultures. It thus represents an Asian initiative in comparative management research, which has long been dominated by the Western initiatives.

I would like to extend my sincere gratitude to many people in Hong Kong, Singapore and Japan, who have generously contributed their time and have shared their knowledge and experience with me. I am especially indebted to Professor S. Gordon Redding of University of Hong Kong, who had first introduced me to the intricate field of cross-cultural comparative management while supervising my work toward a Ph.D. from 1978 to 1982.

I am grateful to Mr. Peter Sowden of Croom Helm Publishers Ltd., who offered me invaluable assistance and encouragement to put together the pieces of work that I had compiled over the last four years. My special thanks must go to City Polytechnic of Hong Kong for funding my research and also to Miss Doris Chi of the Department of Business & Management, who endured many months of word-processing in front of the IBM PC.

Finally, I am deeply indebted to my wife, Minnet, for her patience and understanding without which I could not possibly have lasted to complete the project.

Kazuo John Fukuda
Hong Kong

Chapter One

INTRODUCTION:
JAPANESE MANAGEMENT - THE PAST, PRESENT AND FUTURE

Japan is a complex nation of 120 million racially-homogeneous people set apart from the industrialized Western countries by its tradition and cultural heritage, yet distanced from the rest of neighboring Asian countries by its incredibly rapid rise to become an economic superpower. Today, Japan's economy accounts for a staggering 10 per cent of world product. As the first non-Western country to enter the post-industrial society, the majority of Japan's labor force today is removed not only from primary pursuits but also from secondary employment and engaged in tertiary activities. In fact, the Japanese no longer live in the Far East but reside in an area which might well be called the Middle West [1]. Japan may thus offer an interesting and potentially useful model not only to the developed countries in the West but also to the newly-industrialized countries in East Asia. Over the last 40 years, the views on Japanese-style management have shifted quite rapidly. In this introductory chapter, we shall first examine various views held within and outside Japan before and after the "Japanese Management Boom" of the late 1970s and early 1980s. We shall then attempt to explain why the Japanese have succeeded and what they are doing to keep their neo-Confucian society as the world's most competitive nation in business.

JAPANESE-STYLE MANAGEMENT BEFORE THE BOOM

Until around 1970, the principles of management, developed overwhelmingly in the American context, had largely been regarded as universalistic. The period to 1970 thus saw the extraordinary enthusiasm of Japanese managers to learn about what they considered the superior American management principles and practices. In this period, Japanese management scholars were critical in their evaluation of the practices of the traditional Japanese-style management, often labelling them as backward, irrational, and pre-industrial [2]. They attempted to persuade Japanese managers to adopt a modern Western approach to management. Yoshino, for example, wrote [3]:

> Not only does Japan's managerial system differ from its counterparts in other highly industrialized nations, but also in many of its aspects, it runs counter to what are considered sound principles of management in the Western world, particularly in the US.
>
> [Yoshino, 1968, p.ix]

Stressing the need to modify Japan's traditional management practices in order to meet the challenge of changing environments, he went on to suggest [4]:

> There is a growing incompatibility between the traditional (Japanese) managerial attitudes and patterns and the evolving environment. This incompatibility is causing a serious diminution in their effectiveness. Recent changes in the corporate environment have eroded many of the elements that had supported the traditional managerial ideologies and practices and made them viable.
>
> [Yoshino, 1968, p.274]

Harbison, writing much earlier and reflecting on this period, made a rash prediction about future economic problems for Japan if Japanese organizations failed to adopt superior Western management practices [5]:

> Unless basic rather than trivial or technical changes in the broad philosophy of organization building are forthcoming, Japan is destinied to fall behind in the ranks of modern industrialized nations.
>
> [Harbison, 1959, p.254]

However, despite all these warnings by
management scholars, Japanese managers made a
self-conscious decision to maintain their own
distinctive system rather than progressively to
adopt a Western model [6]. This important
decision made in the late 1960s, coupled with the
rapid internationalization of Japanese business
during the 1970s, had led to a significant
increase in the amount of cross-cultural research
that attempted to explain the differences between
Japanese and Western management practices. An
early cross-cultural study of managerial values
by Haire and his associates suggested that
management practices were closely linked with
cultural values [7]. To date, much of the
literature on Japanese management asserts that
Japanese practices are different because
Japanese cultural values are different. The
study of Japanese cultural values and their
impact on management practices was given a
theoretical base by several writers in the early
1970s. Chie Nakane - probably the best known and
most influential analyst of Japanese values -
described Japanese society as organic and
vertically related [8]. De Bettignies traced the
origin of some distinctive aspects of
organizational behaviour and management to
child-rearing practices and family structure in
Japan [9]. A major weakness of these early
theorists adopting a value-based or cultural
explanation was their failure to articulate a
model of how general cultural values actually
affected the values of managers and workers [10].
The mid-1970s saw some efforts to strengthen
the earlier theoretical base. England's
extensive studies of managerial values, for
example, showed that Japanese managers had the
most homogeneous value system of all countries
[11]. A study conducted by Harari and Zeira
showed that Japanese workers had similar values
regardless of whether they were working for
Japanese or non-Japanese firms, or whether they
were working in Japan or overseas [12].
Whitehill and Takezawa's survey of Japanese
managers and workers in Japan confirmed their
findings [13].
In the late 1970s, many scholars began to
devote considerable attention to more systematic
comparative analysis of management practices as
affected by cultural values, with a prime focus
on Japanese overseas operations, particularly in

the US. (Several studies revealed that Japanese firms operating in the US, when compared with local US firms, showed fewer distinctive characteristics than Japanese firms operating in Japan) [14]. These studies had shown the Japanese firms' efforts to modify their management practices to suit a Western environment. While Japanese firms in Japan, on the whole, remained distinctively Japanese, they adapted their practices abroad employing fewer features of the traditional Japanese-style management. In other words, the national culture affected management practices to a considerable degree, but the culture of a host country seemed to predominate over that of the mother country. This period witnessed the beginning of the boom in publication on Japanese management. It also coincided with the undisputed recognition of Japan as an economic superpower.

JAPAN'S RISE TO AN ECONOMIC SUPERPOWER

Direct investment is the type of investment which aims at participating in actual business undertakings; for instance, the investment to set up a factory overseas, the investment to set up a branch office overseas, or the investment to purchase company shares in order to get directly involved in the management of the issuing companies, are all included in this category. This is in contrast to indirect investment that is portfolio investment, such as purchasing shares or bonds issued by foreign governments or private enterprises, in order to receive dividends or interest payable on those intruments or profits from transactions in those intruments.

Japan's direct overseas investment started on a small scale in the early 1950s. Its volume grew only gradually during the 1950s and 60s. It made a big jump in the early 1970s when Japan started showing an almost embarrassingly large foreign-exchange surplus - the first boom for overseas investment. Japanese companies found it advantageous to operate overseas due to the re-evaluation of the yen after what the Japanese called the "Nixon Shock". By the end of fiscal year 1974, more than US$2 billion had been committed to direct investment in the US alone [15]. Later in the mid-1970s, the mood cooled down somewhat, due to the recession of the

Japanese economy caused by the first "Oil Shock" of 1973.

The second surge of overseas investment occurred in the early 1980s, following serious trade conflicts with the US and Europe. Interestingly, the second boom was marked by the undervalued yen. At the end of 1981, the outstanding balance of the US-to-Japan and Japan-to-the US direct investment was reversed, and the total amount of Japanese investment in the US exceeded that of the US investment in Japan [16]. The move into the US of Japanese manufacturers, led by the big car makers, assumed the proportion of a big boom. Since Honda Motor, with assembly plants in 60 countries, had started the production of the compact car ACCORD in 1982 at its plant in Ohio, other major car makers followed suit to build "Made in US" Japanese cars in places like Tennessee (Nissan Motor) and California (Toyota Motor). Likewise, Japan's leading electronics firms have made a large sum of investment on American soil. A long list of these firms includes SONY in California, Sanyo in Arkansas, Hitachi in Texas, NEC in Massachusetts, and Mitsubishi in North Carolina. Across the Atlantic Ocean, the UK has attracted the largest number of Japanese companies in Western Europe; they are engaged in manufacturing, trading, banking, transport, resources, insurance, and other commercial activities. "Oriental Magic in Welsh Valleys", proclaimed the Financial Times, describing the result of Japanese investments in Wales by SONY, Matsushita, Sekisui Chemicals and so on [17].

Japan has now entered into the third boom as a result of 50 per cent appreciation of the yen since September 1985. Having become stronger in terms of capital and technology and driven by the desire to avoid trade frictions, Japanese companies are at present accelerating the mounting tide of advance into the US, the UK, and other countries, including many in East Asia.

As recently as 1984, the US led with $915 billion, in terms of gross external assets held abroad, followed by Britain with $712 billion, Japan's $341 billion, and West Germany's $234 billion. And, in terms of net external assets, Britain led with $85 billion, followed by Japan's $74 billion, West Germany's $33 billion, and the US net assets of $28 billion. However by the end of 1985, Japan's external assets totalled $438 billion, while its liabilities amounted to $308 billion. The net external assets of $130 billion represented a sharp increase of $56 billion or 74 per cent from the previous year. Japan's Finance Ministry reported comparable figures at $116 billion for Britain and $65 billion for West Germany; the US had net liabilities of $140 billion. Japan thus became the world's largest net creditor nation, moving past Britain into the top spot among the international investors [18]. At the end of 1986, Japan's gross assets in other countries totalled $727 billion, while liabilities amounted to $547 billion. That left Japan with net external assets of $180 billion, up 39 per cent over the previous year [19]. Although comparable figures are not available, Japan is likely to stay as the world's largest overseas creditor nation for the second straight year. Its major external assets included $258 billion in foreign bonds and stocks (up $112 billion from 1985) and $58 billion in direct investments overseas (up $14 billion).

The Fortune's Directory of the Biggest Industrial Corporations Outside the US for 1987 included 152 Japanese firms in the International 500 List (the most for any nation), followed by Britain with 72 and West Germany with 53. Many of the best-known companies such as Nissan, Honda, NEC, and Sony, which are all placed on the Top 100 International List, have been operating their overseas plants with a great degree of success for several years now. With the projected overseas investment surplus of $500 billion by 1992, Japan's economic and financial clout could possibly rival the power held by Britain in the 19th century and the US after World War [20]. In fact, during the 15-month period leading up to April 1987, the total capitalization of the Tokyo Stock Exchange surged from $900 billion to $2.7 trillion (or about 36 per cent of the world stock market capitalizations), which was about $8 billion higher than the US exchanges - London trailing in the third position with a capitalization of $440 billion.

Scholars and managers alike were compelled to scrutinize Japan's strategies, policies, and management practices in order to unravel the underlying reasons for the success and thus find ways to counter what they felt was the Japanese intrusion into their stronghold in both domestic and international markets. While some people, especially the practitioners of management, have long remained rather skeptical that whatever has grown in a cultural and socio-economic system as unique as the one in Japan can offer much that is useful in the context of various Western countries, the accelerating pace of direct investments by Japanese companies and the success of these ventures have led many to conclude that the Japanese must have done something right. Toward the end of the 1970s, it became a general consensus that that something is largely managerial. Fueled by numerous books and papers on Japanese management, a countless number of lectures and seminars were held to learn something from Japan's success. It is interesting to note that the enthusiasm of Western managers to learn more about Japanese management practices at this time seemed to match that of Japanese managers to learn about Western management practices in the late 1950s and 1960s. Japanese management became one of the biggest fads in the Western management circle.

THE HEAT AND ICE ON JAPANESE MANAGEMENT

Just like most other fads, the Japanese management fever started showing a sign of cooling down almost as fast as it had arrived, as very well illustrated by the changing propositions put forward by the authors of several provocative books that had made the best-seller list around the world:

Japan as Number One: Lessons for America

Japan is the world's most effective industrial power that can serve as a model for other developed countries in the West; and we can learn a lot from Japan's success, if we are only willing to pay attention. [21: Vogel, 1979]

Theory Z: How American Business Can Meet the Japanese Challenge

Japanese lessons can be learned, transplanted successfully, and work equally well for our own companies, as clearly demonstrated by Type Z companies, i.e. the successful companies which have many characteristics similar to companies in Japan. [22: Ouchi, 1981]

The Art of Japanese Management: Applications for American Executives

The attributes generally assigned to Japanese success are in fact culture-free and universally shared by many outstanding companies in the West as well as in Japan; and these best-run companies link their purposes and ways of realizing them to human value just as much as to economic measures like profit and efficiency. [23: Pascale and Athos, 1981]

In Search of Excellence: Lessons from America's Best-run Companies

Successful companies in the West share some but not all the characteristics associated with Japanese companies; and our way of management is just as good as the Japanese way or even better. [24: Peters and Waterman, 1982]

The shift in views on Japanese management has been so sweeping that the Japanese themselves are now taking another hard look at the much-cherished ingredients of their economic success. For example, the life-time employment and seniority-based salaries/promotions systems, which characterize Japan's traditional way of management, imply that all regular employees can receive higher positions and salaries as they reach appropriate levels. This is easily accomplished in a growing company and an expanding economy. But problems occur when the economy can no longer absorb the expanding cadre of middle and upper-level managers. Faced with rising expenses and burdened with an aging work-force, even some of the large Japanese companies have started reducing their excess labor through earlier retirement and alternative career paths that increasingly incorporate certain aspects of compensation directly related to an individual's merit.

According to a survey conducted in October 1986 by the Ministry of International Trade and Industry, Japan's large industries have cut back an unprecedented number of jobs - more than

20,000 since autumn 1985 - and are facing their largest labor surplus since the war. The number of jobless then stood at 1.61 million for a record unemployment rate of 2.8 per cent. The figure rose further to 3.2 per cent in May 1987 - the highest since the government began taking data in 1953. While that level is low by the standards of most other industrialized nations, it is a cause for alarm in Japan, which has long prided itself on virtual full employment. It is predicted that increased investments by Japanese companies in production facilities overseas to counter trade friction and the effect of the higher yen could cause the loss of up to 600,000 jobs in Japan by the end of this century.

The recent change in the Japanese economy signals a distinct departure from the past, causing a big headache for the government officials and businessmen alike. Prime Minister Nakasone, warned of worsening unemployment, has formed and decided to head up a special task force himself to study ways of easing the impact of the high yen on employment and finding alternative jobs for thousands of workers who have lost or will lose their jobs.

Peter Drucker, a long-time observer of Japanese management, has also expressed some reservation about the fragile economy of Japan by pointing out a declining growth rate, creeping unemployment which is concealed under the lifetime employment system, a rising deficit in national budget, and the rapid aging of the population. Back in 1982, four years before the arrival of a new economic crisis and the government's subsequent introduction of major programs to restructure Japan's economy, Drucker quite correctly predicted that "clouds are forming over the Japanese sun." [25]

The West's once-torrid love affair with Japanese management appears to be on its way out. It is not that the Japanese methods and techniques do not work for a simultaneous improvement in labor productivity and product quality, which is often regarded as a hall-mark of Japanese management at home and abroad. They have actually worked in many instances; and many people are still convinced that they will continue to work. But there have been so many problems in transplanting Japanese management practices that the Western managers are now casting a harder eye and becoming more choosy

9

about what they should borrow from the Japanese.

Riding high on the tide of shifting views on Japanese management, a recently-published book "The False Promise of Japanese Miracle" even attempts to shatter the illusion of Japan's management supremacy by disproving the theory that Western businesses must adopt Japanese management methods and techniques in order to meet the Japanese challenge [26]. While recognizing that some of the Japanese practices can be beneficial in the West, the book seriously questions the wisdom of adopting the Japanese management system as the cure that will transform companies, plagued by declining productivity and quality, into lean and competitive organizations. The authors give a stern warning that a blind imitation by Western companies would be misguided and inevitably fail. They go so far as to say that the Japanese have achieved their economic miracle by adroitly manipulating the rules of international trade to their own advantage. The crux of their message is that Western countries must become more aggressive in correcting the inequities in the rules by which the Japanese operate in the international markets; and, in dealing with the Japanese, the Western negotiators should employ all the tactics of the Orient, which include making vague and outlandish demands and projecting the image of negotiating from strength.

There is a fresh realization among Western managers that the application of appropriate management practices must be solidly rooted in their own national culture. The importance of gaining a better understanding of the role of culture in influencing management practices was confirmed by Kelley and Worthley's cross-cultural study of management [27]. For example, one of the most important differences between Japanese and American companies lies in congruence to the value sets of national culture. Japanese culture is rooted in groupism, whereas American culture is rooted in individualism. People in both countries form groups, but an important criterion for membership tends to be "what I can do for the group" in the case of the Japanese and "what the group can do for me" in the case of the Americans. The difference is that the Americans have built their society upon individual personalities and the Japanese upon groups. To the Americans, self-reliant individual performance is the ideal. To the Japanese, strengths lie in individual self-sacrifice and conformity to the group. Individual enterprise and the achievement of wealth or fame on independent terms continue to be highly honored by the Americans. By contrast, the great majority of the Japanese find it almost impossible to conceive that an individual can achieve true stature and success except as part of the group he belongs to [28].

The strength of Japanese business organizations can be attributed to the existence of the organizational culture that avoids the cult of individualism, builds group loyalty and mutual support systems, and provides an environment which encourages individual employees to excel and give their best to the organization. But the introduction of the group-oriented values and creation of such organizational culture may be doomed to failure in the culture that values individual initiative, self-reliance, and enlightened self-interest. In other words, beyond a certain point, the totally group-oriented management style runs counter to the American ethos of individualism and ceases to be beneficial.

FROM THE COPYCAT TO THE CREATIVE INNOVATOR

For over a century, the Japanese have followed the West in such industries as shipbuilding, steel, cameras, automobiles, and electronics - always elaborating, modifying, and refining the original work brilliantly. Today, memory chips, VCRs, even personal computers, are produced in high volume; and Japan's brilliance has usually come in the improvement of technology and the perfection of manufacturing. One estimate shows that the ratio of borrowed foreign technology to home-grown technology during Japan's post-war growth period has been twenty to one in favor of borrowed technology [29]. For one thing, Japan so far has won only four Nobel prizes in science, compared with 142 for the US.

Many visitors to Japan have said, "I could not find any new ingredients, but the Japanese sure know how to cook better." Some Japanese also say that their society, viewed from the outside, must appear like a "black hole" in the sky of the world. Culturally shrunken to the point of maximum density, Japan does reveal tremendous surges of energy, but without any transmittal of signals. It is a "receiver", rather than a "transmitter", civilization [30]. To put it simply, Japan has achieved its current level of economic success not by being a creative innovator but rather by being an effective borrower.

Though they have long been a heavy borrower of ideas and knowhow from other cultures, the Japanese have always managed to keep their own identity. Convinced of the uniqueness of their subtle and complex culture, the Japanese believe that no one who was not born and reared in Japanese society can ever truly become part of it. They also believe that their racial homogeneity and sense of commonality are among Japan's strengths and reasons for achieving its economic success. However, a fair number of Japanese are concerned that the continued borrowings from other cultures may dilute these inherent strengths. This may at least partly explain why Japan today still remains largely as a closed society. In a way, the new affluence, built upon years of self-denial and toil, has knocked the Japanese slightly off balance. While a new debate looms on whether Japan should become an open society by playing a more active diplomatic and military role befitting its economic superpower status, some Japanese are even worried that they are already heading into decline.

In spite of their worries, prosperity today is changing things for better. As they grow more affluent, the Japanese are at last getting over their long-held inferiority complex toward the West. It is true that scholarly work in modern Japan has been mostly devoted to absorbing knowledge from abroad and synthesizing it with what is already known; industry has stressed the learning and adaptation of existing technologies rather than the creation of new ones. One may consider that this situation is natural in a country like Japan, which has only recently come into close contact with the rest of the world and has been engrossed in the task of catching up.

Reischauer, a professor of Japanese history and culture at Harvard University and the US Ambassador to Japan from 1961 to 1966, once noted that [31]:

> There is reason to wonder if intellectual creativeness will ever be a special forte of the Japanese .... the Japanese have always seemed to lean more toward subtlety and sensitivity than to clarity of analysis, to intuition rather than reason, to pragmatism rather than the theory, to organizational skills rather than greater intellectual concepts.
>
> [Reischauer, 1977, p.226]

He also pointed out that the traits of great success in practical applications but relative weakness in theoretical innovation were also the characteristics of the US during its period of catching up with Europe. Nevertheless, such a characterization of the Japanese may explain why the Westerners tend to look on a relative lack of intellectual creativity as a sign of inferiority.

Increasingly the Japanese feel stung by foreign criticism that they are the copycat borrower of technologies. They also fear that in the face of their own extraordinary success in adapting borrowed technologies, an increasingly impatient West will start limiting Japan's access to new technologies. As the country has already closed the gap with the West in many science and technology-related fields, its leaders in government, business and education are now trying to stir up a cyclone of innovation in the very way the Japanese think and behave. Japan has more than 15,000 scientists and engineers studying in the US alone. They are trying to learn as much about "how" their counterparts do research as about "what" they are doing. Private companies are sending platoons to the US for first-hand experience of developing new technologies in which the US still has a competitive edge over Japan. For example, Japanese software engineers are in residence at Carnegie Group, a Pittsburgh artificial intelligence company. Similarly, the Japan Science and Technology Agency's innovative Exploratory Research for Advanced Technology program has brought in Americans, Europeans, and Asians to work for a 5-year stint with Japanese researchers at universities and in national research institutes [32].

Under the new national slogan "Change or Perish", the Japanese are determined to win the race to close the creativity gap with the West. This is by no means a simple task in a culture that values conformity and ability to work within group more highly than individuality. Yet Japan's drive to become a more creative innovator is evident in an impressive base of human resources. The country has one of the world's largest scientific and engineering workforces. It graduates more than 70,000 engineers annually - twice as many per capita as the US. It has nearly 500,000 scientists and engineers engaged in research - almost a numerical match for the Americans engaged in non-military projects. Twenty years ago, Japan spent only 1.6 per cent of its Gross National Product (GNP) on science and technology research - the lowest among major industrialized countries. However, according to an annual survey report compiled by the Management and Coordination Agency, that figure shot up to 2.8 per cent, or $55.6 billion, in fiscal 1985. In comparison, the US spent 2.7 per cent of its GNP, or $162.2 billion, including research for military applications, during the same period. Research expenditures in the private sector did not differ much between the two countries. Japan ranked third after the Soviet Union and West Germany in percentage of GNP spent on research in science and technology-related fields, but was second only to the US in the total amount spent.

BREAK FROM TRADITIONS

In the past, the Japanese followed the world. For the longest time, they believed that the clearest expression of universal truths about civilized man was to be found in the ancient Chinese ethic of Confucianism - perhaps the most significant import that has left a lasting effect on the Japanese system of thought to date. In more recent years, they recognized the superiority of the Western technologies and adapted them willingly and eagerly to their own use in order to catch up with the West. Although the Japanese today show a strong desire and determination to become the innovators and thus lead the world in a few carefully selected fields, they have not stopped searching for new ideas, methods, and techniques that they can borrow from others. Whereas many people in the West still continue to talk about the merits of Japanese-style management with a strong collective orientation, an increasing number of Japanese are expressing a serious concern about the demerits of just such management. Indeed, some Japanese companies have already broken away from their management traditions and started to adopt a more Western-style of management [33].

It is a time-honored practice in Japan for the leader to take the brunt of responsibility for any serious mistake made by his subordinates, even if he personally had nothing to do with the wrongdoing. For example, following the surfacing of reports in April 1987 of the sale of restricted high technologies by its subsidiary to the Soviet Union, the two top executives (i.e. Chairman and President) of Toshiba Corp. - Japan's second biggest electronic machinery manufacturer - announced their decision to quit the job. Still, their choice of new president was accepted, and both were subsequently asked to remain as advisors to Toshiba Corp.

In Japan, as is often done in the West, the Chief Executive Officer (CEO) can be legally ousted by stockholders. However, in practice, this is rarely done because of potential damage to the company's image. The 1982 "Mitsukoshi Incident", which involved the ousting of the powerful reigning CEO of the largest department store group in Japan, was therefore a startling event in modern Japan's business history. The CEO was blamed, among others, for the use of the traditional system of decision-making by consensus to disguise poorly planned merchandising and promotion policies. Kanebo - a large manufacturer of textiles, cosmetics, medicine, food products, and housing - has also gone through a less drastic but equally significant change. The company had long been run with a strong emphasis on group harmony. Strict adherence to promotions based on seniority, however, had resulted in a cumbersome organization with a slow and awkward decision-making process, and the diffusion of accountability and responsibility. To overcome these problems and compete more squarely with younger and more aggressive companies, Kanebo in 1984 decided to reorganize the management team and, for the first time in its history, appointed a female director to the board - a bold break from the Japanese management tradition. These two recent events at the leading Japanese companies are significant for they reflect a changing environment in which the practices of traditional Japanese management may no longer be effective.

Attempts to break away from the tradition are being made even more vigorously by Japanese companies operating abroad. For example, there are well over 800 Japanese companies established in Hong Kong, and they are involved in practically all sectors of economic activities. Japan's direct investment in Hong Kong, amounting to over $2.9 billion on a cumulative basis as of March 1986, comprises 3.5 per cent of its total direct overseas investment - the seventh largest destination in the world, and second largest in East Asia after Indonesia [34]. Despite the heavy investment inflow to Hong Kong, opinions about Japanese businesses among the local population remain unfavorable. A recent survey of business students aged between 18 and 20 revealed that given a choice of employment in either an American or a Japanese firm, only one out of 10 would prefer the Japanese [35]. When asked about the competitiveness of salaries, the prospect for promotions, and the scope of training/development programs, the favorable opinions expressed by the respondents were roughly 90 per cent for American firms and 60 per cent for Japanese firms.

Such a finding clearly illustrates a serious problem that Japanese firms in Hong Kong are having in attracting the qualified college graduates. Perhaps, the root of problem is located in the wholesale export of the national and organizational culture intact from Japan. It is also to be noted that the top management positions at Japanese companies operating in Hong Kong are invariably occupied by the Japanese executives sent in directly from the headquarters and most of these executives stay at the post only for three years, on the average. As a result, the vast majority of them are slow to recognize the cultural differences and reluctant to make any radical changes to their practices of management. However, an increasing number of firms, especially those run by the top executives who have stayed longer in Hong Kong, are beginning to question the wisdom of employing their own home-grown practices of management on foreign soil.

Recognizing the problem as potentially a dangerous barrier to their future growth, some Japanese firms operating in Hong Kong have already decided to adopt a more Western style of management to attract and retain their local management talents. Instead of simply complaining about a total lack of their local employees' loyalty to the company, the executives in these firms are now trying to understand the relatively more individual-oriented values of Hong Kong Chinese culture and accept the differences. For example, several large trading and retailing firms, which employ a relatively large number of locals, have introduced the merit-based salaries and promotions system. One such firm with over 25 years of business operation in Hong Kong has only recently announced a new policy to localize its management by promoting the qualified employees to senior management positions as high as the Deputy Managing Director.

A MODEL FOR OTHERS ?

Several countries in East Asia - from South Korea in the North to Singapore in the South - are increasingly using Japan as a conscious model for their economic development. South Korea, Taiwan, Hong Kong, and Singapore are now called Asian NICs (Newly Industrialized Countries) or the "Four Little Dragons", Japan being the "Big Dragon". During the 1960s and 1970s, the national economies of Japan and the four Asian NICs, as a group, outstripped all others in the average growth rates of Gross National Product (GNP) per capita - nearly 7.6 per cent compared to around 2 per cent for the leading OECD countries [36]. Over the first half of this decade, Asian NICs achieved an average increase of 6.8 per cent in GNP, while the world average of non-oil producing developing countries showed only a 2.4 per cent increase during the same period [37]. Table 1-1 shows the selected indicators of Japan and four Asian NICs.

Table 1-1: Selected Indicators of East Asian
          Countries

	Population, 1986 (million)	Per Capita GNP, 1986 (US$)	Average GNP Growth, 1981-86 (per cent)
Japan	120.0	11,080	5.30
S. Korea	43.0	1,889	7.75
Taiwan	20.0	3,100	6.93
Hong Kong	6.0	6,173	5.67
Singapore	2.6	7,200	4.57

Source: Drexel Burnham Lambert (HK) Ltd., July
        1987

The phenomenal economic growth of the past is likely to continue. The World Bank projects that the annual growth rate of Asian NICs for the rest of this century will be 7 per cent on the average. This estimate suggests that the economy of Asian NICs will grow two or three times faster than industrial countries such as the US and the European Community (EC). According to a report published in 1985 by Japan's Council for Economic Research in the Pacific Region, by year 2000, Hong Kong will develop to a level near par with the EC in terms of per capita GNP (about US$13,000), whereas Singapore will by then surpass the EC. The report also said Japan would become equal to the US (about $19,000) within fifteen years. It must be added that this estimation was calculated on the basis of the exchange rate that prevailed back in 1982. Therefore, as a result of 50 per cent appreciation of the yen since September 1985, Japan's per capita GNP has already surpassed that of the the US, if the current exchange rate (US$1 = 125 yen) is applied.

In its 1986 report comparing 31 industrialized nations, the Geneva-based European Management Forum stated that Japan had replaced the US as the world's most competitive nation in business. The report also named Taiwan as the

most competitive, with Singapore second and Hong
Kong third, among nine NICs. The nation's
competitiveness in business is obviously affected
by the government's economic policies,
government-business relationships, education, and
technologies. It is also much influenced by the
nation's socio-cultural factors. Hofheinz and
Calder directed attention to the role of cultural
values in economic development, by pointing out
that Japan and Asian NICs have in common a
cultural tradition of Confucianism [38]. Kahn
has also suggested that the recent economic
success of these East Asian countries is due in
large part to certain cultural traits shared by
the majority of people in these countries and
attributable to an upbringing in the Confucian
tradition [39]. Though there are no doubt variations in their respective interpretations of
Confucianism, certain common denominators remain
significant. Kahn isolated the following:

* Socialization within the family unit.
* A tendency to help the group.
* A sense of hierarchy.
* A sense of complementarity of relations.

Hofstede's cross-cultural study on work-related
values of managers has provided a strong support
for Kahn's contention that such traits are
salient in neo-Confucian society [40].
    The critics of neo-Confucian society argued
that this type of organization was inflexible and
unresponsive to external changes. They contended
that the Confucianism of East Asia was an
insuperable barrier to modernization. As the
first country to prove them wrong, Japan has
developed what some call a "high energy"
Cofucianism, that produces hyperactivity, not
stagnation, and unswerving momentum rather than
immovable inertia [41]. Japan has thus shown the
world and, especially its neighouring countries
in East Asia, that Confucian or neo-Confucian, to
be more accurate, values are not barriers to
industrialization but, suitably modified, can
actually become the foundation of successful
modern business organization.

NOTES

1. Burks, A.W., _Japan: Profile of a Postindustrial Power_, Boulder, Colorado: Westview Press, (1981)

2. Odaka, K., "Traditionalism, Democracy in Japanese Industry", _Industrial Relations_, (1963), vol.3, no.1, pp.95-103; Yamada, T., "Japanese management practices - Change is on the way as traditional habits are challenged", _Conference Board Record_, (1969), vol.6, no.11, pp.22-23

3. Yoshino, M.Y., _Japan's Managerial System: Tradition and Innovation_, Cambridge, Mass.: MIT Press (1968)

4. ibid.

5. Harbison, F., "Management in Japan" in F. Harbison and C.A. Myers (eds.), _Management in the Industrial World: An International Analysis_, New York: McGraw Hill, (1959), pp.259-264

6. Dunphy, D.C., "An Historical Review of the Literature on the Japanese Enterprise and its Managment" in S.R. Clegg, D.C. Dunphy, and S.G. Redding (eds.), _The Enterprise and Management in East Asia_, Hong Kong: Center of Asian Studies (1986), pp.343-368

7. Haire, M., E.E. Ghiselli, and L.W. Porter, _Managerial Thinking: An International Study_, New York: John Wiley & Sons, (1966)

8. Nakane, C., _Japanese Society_, London: Weidenfeld & Nicolson, (1970)

9. De Bettignies, H.C., "Japanese Organizational Behaviour: A Psychocultural Approach" in D. Graves (ed.), _Managerial Research: A Cross-Cultural Perspective_, New York: Jossey Bass Inc., (1971), pp.15-93

10. Dunphy, D.C., (1986), op.cit.

11. England, G.W., _The Manager and His Values: An International Perspective from the United States, Japan, Korea, India and Australia_, Cambridge, Mass.: Ballinger, (1975)

12. Harari, E, and Y. Zeira, "Morale Problems in Non-American Multinational Corporations in the United States", _Management International Review_, (1974), vol.14, no.6, pp.43-57

13. Whitehill, A.M., and S. Takezawa, "Workplace Harmony: Another Japanese Miracle?", _Columbia Journal of World Business_, (1978), vol.13, no.3, pp.25-39

14. Pascale, R.T., "Communication and Decison-making Across Cultures: Japanese and American Comparisons", <u>Administrative Science Quarterly</u>, (1978), vol.23, no.1, pp.91-110; Cook, N.E., "Human Resource Management Style: A Comparative Study of Japanese and American Banks in California", Ph.D. thesis (UCLA, 1978), Ann Arbor, Mich.: University Microfilms International

15. Kraar, L., "The Japanese are coming with their own style of management", <u>Fortune</u>, (March 1975), pp.116-121 & pp.160-164

16. <u>The Oriental Economist</u>, (Sept. 1983), "Japanese-style Management on Trial in America", pp.8-13

17. <u>The Financial Times</u>, (21 January 1977), "Oriental Magic in Welsh Valleys", p.11

18. <u>Business News</u>, (South China Morning Post, 28 May 1986), "Japan takes over as top creditor", p.10

19. <u>Business News</u>, (South China Morning Post, 27 May 1987), "Japan's External Assets Rise", p.8

20. <u>Time</u>, (March 18, 1985), "Global Money Machine", pp.38-40

21. Vogel, E.F., <u>Japan as Number One: Lessons for America</u>, Cambridge, Mass.: Harvard University Press, 1979

22. Ouchi, W.G., <u>Theory Z: How American business can meet the Japanese challenge</u>, New York: Avon Books, (1981)

23. Pascale, R.T., and A.G. Athos, <u>The Art of Japanese Management: Applications for American Executives</u>, New York: Simon & Schuster, (1981)

24. Peters, T.J., and R.H. Waterman, <u>In Search of Excellence: Lessons from America's Best-run Companies</u>, New York: Harper & Row (1982)

25. Drucker, P., "Clouds forming over the Japanese sun", <u>Wall Street Journal</u>, (July 13, 1982)

26. Sethi, S.P., N. Namiki, and C.L. Swanson, <u>The False Promise of Japanese Miracle</u>, London: Pitman, (1984)

27. Kelley, L., and R. Worthley, "The Role of Culture in Comparative Management: A Cross-cultural Perspective", <u>Academy of Management Journal</u>, (1981), vol.24, no.1, pp.164-173

28. Christopher, R.C., <u>The Japanese Mind</u>, London: Pan Books, (1984)

29. Odiorne, G.S., "The Trouble with Japanese Management System", <u>Business Horizon</u>, (Jul./Aug. 1984), pp.17-23

30. Burks, A.W., (1981), op.cit.

31. Reischauer, E.O., _The Japanese_, Tokyo: Charles E. Tuttle Co., (1977)

32. _Fortune_, (30 March 1987), "Trying to Transcend Copycat Science", pp.38-42

33. Yang, C.Y., "Demystifying Japanese Management Practices", _Harvard Business Review_, (Nov./Dec. 1984), pp.172-182

34. Matsuura, K., "Japan's Overseas Investment and Hong Kong", mimeograph, Japan Information and Cultural Office, (Hong Kong, March 1987)

35. Project Report, "Opinion Survey of American and Japanese Businesses in Hong Kong", unpublished students' report, City Polytechnic of Hong Kong, (1984)

36. _World Bank_, World Development Report, (1981)

37. Matsuura, K., "Future of the East Asia Economy and the Roles of Hong Kong and Japan", Paper presented at the Rotary Club of Penninsula meeting (Hong Kong, 19 May 1987)

38. Hofheinz, R., and K.E. Calder, _The East Asia Edge_, New York: Basic Books, (1982)

39. Kahn, H., _World Economic Development: 1979 and Beyond_, London: Croom Helm, (1979)

40. Hofstede, G., _Culture's Consequences: International Differences in Work-related Values_, Beverly Hills, Calif.: Sage Publications, (1984)

41. Sayle, M., "High Energy Brand of Confucianism", _Far Eastern Economic Review_, (30 April 1987), p.47

Chapter Two

COMPARATIVE MANAGEMENT: WHAT ARE THE ISSUES?

It is impossible to study anything without at least implicitly comparing it with something else.   Comparative analysis is a shift away from concentration on a unique organization, country, or culture toward seeking generalization about patterns of relationships in a variety of settings.   Cross-cultural comparative management studies look at business organizations and their management in various cultural settings.   In recent years, an increasing number of researchers in the field have stated that the studies should describe organizational behavior within countries and cultures, compare organizational behavior across countries and cultures, and, perhaps most importantly, seek to understand and improve the interactions of co-workers from different countries and cultures [1]. In this chapter, we shall examine two important issues in the study of comparative management - the universality of theories and the transferability of practices. In addition, the concept of culture will be examined to better equip ourselves for a meaningful comparative analysis of management across cultures.

APPROACHES TO COMPARATIVE MANAGEMENT STUDY

Comparative management study is largely a post-World War II phenomenon, emerging as a distinctive discipline only around 1960. Numerous attempts have been made since to build conceptual foundations which could provide a useful framework for the examination and explanation of management similarities and differences across cultures.   In spite of the very recent origin, there is already a considerable diversity in the theoretical underpinning of the discipline, leading to what

Schollhammer calls the "Comparative Management Theory Jungle" [2]. The concepts and method-ological approaches used by researchers can be divided roughly into three groups: the economic development approach, the environmental approach, and the behavioral approach [3].

The economic development approach, first undertaken in the 1950s, traced the initial large-scale projects on industrialization of developing countries. It was essentially a macro approach, concentrating on the basic trends of managerial development rather than analysis of specific management practices at the micro level. During the 1960s, using the economic development concern as a main premise, the environmental approach attempted to highlight the impact of external environmental factors (e.g. socio-economic, political-legal, technological, educational, and cultural) on management practices and effectiveness. This is still essentially a macro approach with the underlying hypothesis that the managerial practices and effectiveness are the functions of external environmental factors. Toward the end of the 1960s, the behavioral approach in cross-cultural comparative management studies began to be increasingly employed to explain behavioral patterns of individuals and groups in organizational settings. This is a micro approach, with the underlying hypothesis that attitudes, value systems, and need hierarchies are the functions of a given culture. By establishing relationships between these concepts and managerial practices and effectiveness, researchers have attempted to deduce the impact of cultural variables on management practices and effectiveness.

The grouping of various orientations into these three approaches may bring some order into the Comparative Management Theory jungle. However, the problem of evaluating the approaches is a little like the exercise of looking at an elephant - what one sees depends on one's vantage point [4]. There are distinct differences in emphasis among them as well as substantial similarities. Also, each approach has its own merits and drawbacks. With the economic development thrust given in the first approach, the cross-cultural management field did not progress far beyond identifying and noting the importance of managerial input in economic development. The over-emphasis on external factors given by the environmental approach has often led to the belief that individual enterprises are basically passive agents of external environments. The claim made by the behaviorists of a linkage between culture and management has also raised doubts about the ill-defined concepts and poorly-conceived operational measures of the concepts themselves.

It appears that the differences among the three approaches are partially caused by semantic differences in the definition of comparative management as a body of knowledge and the tendency of scholars to avoid talking to each other or trying to understand each other. It would, therefore, be important to minimize the existing biases of the various orientations by attempting to integrate and synthesize the different approaches for the further advancement of Comparative Management Theory.

QUESTIONS OF UNIVERSALITY OR UNIQUENESS

The basic interest of compapative management study is to gain insights into the universality of management theories and the transferability of management practices [5]. Quite naturally, then, one issue which has been receiving a great deal of attention in comparative management study is the question of universality or uniqueness of management across cultures. The argument persists between:

* Those who believe that efficient and effective management is largely based on universal principles, practices and knowhow which can be transferred to any culture; and
* Those who advocate that management as philosophy or process is essentially or substantially culture-bound.

In the main, the classical school theorists have argued that management principles are universal and applicable to all types of organizations in all situations. Harbison and Myers, for example, maintained that there was a general logic of management which had applicability to both developed and developing countries [6]. Similarly, in their approach to the study of comparative management, Koontz and O'Donnell took a position that management fundamentals (i.e. concepts, theories, and principles) had universal applications in every kind of enterprise and at every level of enterprise [7]. They said:

> The principles related to the task of managing apply to any kind of enterprise in any kind of culture. The purpose of different enterprises may vary, but all which are organized do rely on effective group operation for efficient attainment of whatever goals they have ... The fundamental truths (principles) are applicable elsewhere.
> [Koontz, H. and C.O'Donnell, 1968, p.vi]

This sort of universalist view of management, still taken by many management scholars, would suggest a strong tendency toward American parochialism. The vast majority of management schools are in the US; the majority of management professors and researchers are American trained; and the majority of management research focuses on the US. After reviewing over 11,000 articles published in 24 management journals between 1971 and 1980, Adler found that approximately 80 per cent were studies of the US conducted by Americans [8]. Fewer than 5 per cent of the articles, describing the behavior of people in organizations, included the concept of culture. Fewer than 1 per cent focused on the work interaction of people from one or more cultures. In spite of such long-established parochialism in the field of management, the domain of business is rapidly moving beyond national boundaries.

An increasing number of cross-cultural management researchers have, in fact, begun to challenge the contention of the universalists taking a rather parochial view. Oberg, from his overseas experience and empirical research, concluded that [9]:

> Cultural differences from one country to another are more significant than many writers appear to recognize. If management principles are to be truly

universal, they must face up to the challenge of other cultures and other business climates. The universalist claim is hardly warranted by either evidence or intuition at this stage in the development of management theory.

[Oberg, W., 1963, p.141]

He argued that the applicability of management principles was limited to a particular culture and that it might be fruitless to search for a common set of principles, absolutes, or determinate solutions. A similar view was expressed by Bedeian, who had observed that different cultures possessed different organizational norms and behavior standards and that they recognized these as legitimate forms of influence [10].

There are other studies which have similarly adopted this environmental approach in examining the relationship between culture and management. Most of them have pointed out the need to take account of the impact of culture and other extenal environmental factors on management process and effectiveness. Farmer and Richman, for example, maintain that most studies of management have taken place within a "black box" labeled management, without much concern for the external environment in which the firm operates; as long as the external environment is about the same for all firms, the approach is valid; however, in cases where the environment differs significantly, as is the case between nations, present theory (of management) is inadequate to explain comparative differentials in efficiency [11].

Based on this premise, they proposed a model (see Figure 2-1) to ascertain the influence of external constraints on management process. The general classes of constraints considered by them were educational, sociological, political-legal, and economic characteristics. However, Schollhammer claimed that their model put too much emphasis on the necessity for the management's environmental adaptation and gave too little attention to the fact that the management might choose to act in defiance of certain external constraints [12]. He argued that managers were not necessarily passive agents of external environments. Instead, both an organization and its management interact with environmental stimuli and attempt to mould them in order to achieve goals and objectives.

Figure 2-1: Farmer-Richman's Model of Comparative Management

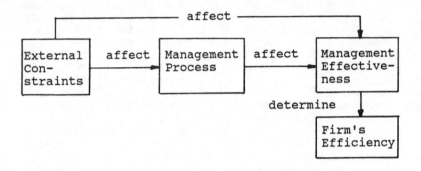

[Farmer, R.N. and B.M. Richman, 1964]

Negandhi and Estafen, adopting more of the behavioral approach in comparative management analysis, have somewhat expanded the Farmer-Richman model by raising a point that management process is dependent on not only the external environmental constraints but also management philosophy [13]. Based on the premise that management philosophy is not necessarily a product of the given culture and environment, as implied in the Farmer-Richman model, they have proposed an alternative model of comparative management (see Figure 2-2). It is Negandhi and Estafen's position that certain areas of management philosophy should be introduced as a variable which may or may not be influenced by external environmental factors. They consider that management philosophy, defined as the expressed or implied attitudes on relationships of a firm with some of its external and internal agents, has a considerable impact on the management process and its effectiveness. Their model also suggests that the environmental factors directly affect not only management practices but also management and enterprise effectiveness. It postulates that management practices are dependent upon external environmental factors and the firm's stance toward its task agents - consumers, employees, suppliers, distributors, stockholders, community, and government.

Figure 2-2: Negandhi-Estafen's Model of
          Comparative Management

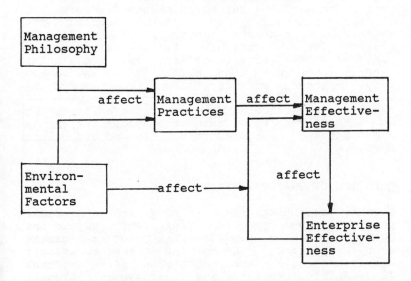

[Negandhi, A.R. and B.D. Estafen, 1965]

The study of managers from 14 countries, conducted by Haire and two other psychologists in the mid-1960s, found that some 28 per cent of the cross-national differences in attitudes and beliefs about management were accounted for by cultural explanations [14]. Hofstede also found highly significant differences in the attitudes and behavior of employees and managers from different countries, who were working in an American multinational company [15]. In his study, national culture explained more of the differences than did position within the organization, profession, age, or gender; 50 per cent of the differences were explained by national culture. The findings from these studies give support both to the universalists and cultural relativists.

Though culture alone cannot be used to explain everything, it still has a considerable influence on managers' attitudes and behavior in different countries. The universal trend toward more complex organizations suggests the importance of starting with the environmental suprasystems as a basis for conducting comparative management studies. Culture is surely one of the key environmental factors; and it is impossible to fully understand the organization and its management apart from a given cultural setting. To be sure, this does not mean that cultural differences are the prime determinants, but they are, without any doubt, very important considerations. In summary, the variables and factors lying outside the organizational boundaries are just as important as the variables within the organization in understanding management practices and effectiveness.

QUESTION OF TRANSFERABILITY

Another important issue rising from the basic interest of comparative management study is the question of the transferability of management across cultures. Management transfer is not complete until the knowledge of management fundamentals received and learned is actually applied in a way which will lead to effective behavior consistent with a given environmental-cum-cultural setting [16]. In other words, the cross-cultural transfer of management involves not only the technical aspect of management, as expressed in basic concepts, theories, and principles, but also a behavioral aspect of management, as observed in the actual performance of management functions. The technical aspect may not be susceptible to cultural variation, but this is hardly the case when the behavioral aspect is involved. As a result, many scholars have conducted research with a special focus on organizational behavior in different cultural settings. They have basically concentrated on three different aspects [17]:

* National character profiles, which are linked
  with certain organizational behavior variables.
* Attitudes and perceptions of managers
  concerning some key management concepts and
  activities.
* Prevalent beliefs, value systems, and need
  hierarchies in a given society.

Roberts' review of cross-cultural studies related
to organizational behavior has revealed that
there are two major groups of researchers in the
field [18]:

* A group interested in the effect of culture on
  individual attitudes or behavior in
  organizations (i.e. Micro-oriented approach)
* A group preoccupied with the effect of culture
  on organization, structural, environmental, and
  transaction variables (i.e. Macro-oriented
  approach)

     Davis, who has adopted the micro-oriented
approach, considers that every culture has a
system of values and it is the unique
constellation and patterning of values that
differentiate people from one another [19].
Culture, in this sense, includes systems of
values; and values are among the blocks of
culture. Thus, one of the critical elements
dealt with in his proposed conceptual framework
is values, which are sets of interrelated ideas,
concepts, and principles to which individuals,
groups, and societies attach strong sentiments.
Values and ideologies are often used
interchangeably, though the latter can be more
specifically defined as the ideas, beliefs, and
modes of thinking held by a group. Values are
abstract, and can be both consciously and
unconsciously held. They are, therefore,
relatively general beliefs that either define
what is right and wrong or specify general
preferences. From this broad mental orientation
develops a set of attitudes - predisposition to
perform, perceive, think, and feel.
     In fact, the cultural orientation of a
society reflects the complex interaction of the
values, attitudes, and behaviors displayed by its
members [20]. As shown in Figure 2-3, individuals
express culture through the values that they hold
about life and the world around them. These
values in turn affect their attitudes about the

31

form of behavior considered most appropriate in
any given situation. The attitudes then provide
the basis for day-to-day behavior by generating
the rules of behavior to be applied to a specific
culture. To be sure, diversity exists within and
between cultures, but within a single culture a
certain form of behavior is favored and others
repressed. The continually changing patterns of
individual and group behavior eventually
influence the society's culture, and the cycle
begins again.

Figure 2-3: The Influence of Culture on Behavior

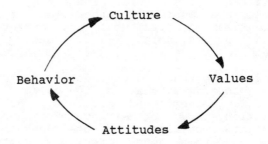

[Adler, N.J., 1986,P.9]

In contrast to the micro-oriented approach,
some researchers have conducted studies to
compare total organizations in different
cultures. For example, Abegglen, in his study of
Japanese firms, observed and interviewed in 53
factories in Japan [21]. The study, an exploratory case study of data aggregated from various
firms, revealed two major factors differentiating
Japanese factories from American factories:

* A lack of differentiation of factory
  organization and other social groups.
* A relative lack of individualization and
  impersonalization in the relationships.

Dore conducted a detailed study of one British
and one Japanese factory to identify different
ways of organizing enterprise [22]. He found
many differences, some of which were parallel to
those noted by Abegglen:

* The workers' families in the British firm have limited contact with the firm; the workers' families in the Japanese firm are peripheral members of the enterprise family.
* In the British firm, managerial staff have titles which directly specify their functions; in the Japanese firm, responsibilities are assigned to groups and can be shunted around among individuals within them.

Do these differences hold true for most Japanese firms or just for some? We could question the validity of generalization to all Japanese firms, which is largely supported by data drawn from sources such as the summaries of organizational statistics.

There are shortcomings associated with the use of either the miro or macro approach to comparative management study. In assessing the state of cross-cultural comparative management research, Richard Peterson - the Chairman of the Academy of Management's International Management Division - has given a long list of the shortcomings of much of research in the field. It includes [23]:

a) Lack of theoretical base -- Neglect to test theoretical or conceptual models to put the study results in a broader framework.

b) Ethnocentrism -- Tendency to adhere to the assumption that companies in other nations should be compared to the Western industrial model.

c) Overemphasis on cultural variance -- Tendency to lose sight of the similarities across nations and neglect to look at variances within a culture (nation).

d) Study limited to one nation -- Inclination to look at the situation in one country without relating the findings to those of other nations.

e) Reliance on a single research method -- Heavy reliance on one method of gaining information (i.e. questionnaires) without the use of supplementary methods such as interviews, participant observation, behavioral scenarios, and so forth.

f)   Imbalance in terms of areas of studies --
     Abundance of studies in a small number
     of Western countries and Japan, but few
     elsewhere, especially in East Asia
     where we are virtually "babes in the
     woods" in understanding both the
     diversity and commonality of organized
     behavior.

PROPOSED MODEL OF COMPARATIVE MANAGEMENT

As discussed earlier, Negandhi and Estafen have,
in effect, proposed the combination of micro and
macro-oriented approaches to cross-cultural
comparative management studies [24]. The
theoretical concept expressed in their model may
be criticized as being not comprehensive enough,
as being arbitrary in the selection of the
various factors included in the model, and as
being superficial in the sense that the focus is
simply on overt managerial behavior as it
manifests itself in a few seemingly randomly
selected relationships with the internal and
external environmental factors. Negandhi-
Estafen's model may also be criticized for not
expressing concern about the causes of a given
behavior. However, in a complex field such as
comparative management, the indicated shortcomings of their approach also give rise to the
following advantages [25]:

*   The concentration on only a few largely
    controllable variables facilitates the
    model's use for empirical investigation.
*   The concentration on management activities and
    managerial behavior facilitates the exami-
    nation of the transferability of the
    behavioral aspect of management across
    cultures.

That their model can lead to meaningful empirical
results has been demonstrated by Estafen's study
in Ch‍ile [26] and Negandhi's study in Taiwan
[27]. Therefore, from the point of view of
conducting a study to determine the transferability of management practices, Negandhi-
Estafen's model of comparative management may
provide a particularly useful framework for a
meaningful comparative analysis of managements
across cultures.

To simplify the task of advancing comparative management theories, it may be useful to divide management practices into three distinctive layers: managing technical core activities, managing the social system in an organization, and managing external relationships [28]. The technical core activities of organizations such as planning and control are, in large part, influenced by technological factors, size, market conditions, and managerial policies. The social system within the organization such as interpersonal relationships may be more dependent on socio-cultural factors, while the external relationships such as establishing legitimacy and inter-organizational relations are considerably influenced by political-legal, and economic factors.

Some writers have suggested that the American management practices in technical core activities are more advanced and others may benefit by learning from the US, while the Japanese and European practices may have some useful lessons for the US with respect to the external relationships of organizations [29].

Managing the social system within the organization remains a twilight zone where much research is still needed. For this very reason, the main focus of our study will be on the social system which is greatly influenced by the nation's socio-cultural factors. A model of comparative management, shown in Figure 2-4, is therefore proposed here in order to pursue our study on the transferability of the Japanese-style management practices. Our model incorporates Negandhi-Estafen's model (see Figure 2-2) to a large degree, but the influence of organizational culture is emphasized.

Over the last few years, managers and scholars alike have come to recognize the importance of organizational culture as climate creator. Organizational culture is what the organization has learned as a total social unit over the course of its history. It may be defined as follows [30]:

> Organizational culture is the pattern of
> basic assumptions that a given group has
> invented, discovered, or developed in
> learning to cope with its problems of
> external adaptation and internal
> integration - a pattern of assumptions
> that has worked well enough to be
> considered valid and, therefore, to be
> taught to new members as the correct way
> to perceive, think, and feel in relation
> to those problems.
>
> [Schein, E.H., 1983, p.14]

Figure 2-4: Proposed Comparative Management Model

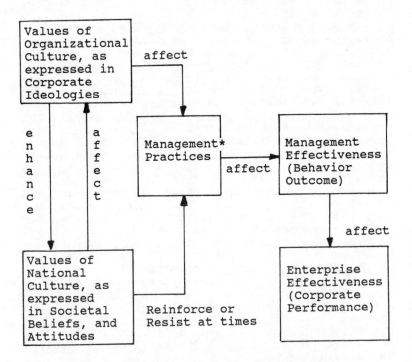

* Note: The practices employed in managing the
  "social system" in an organization.

The external and internal problems, shown in Table 2-1, are always intertwined and acting simultaneously. The model of organizational culture that then emerges is one of shared solutions to these problems which work well enough to be taken almost for granted.

Table 2-1: External and Internal Problems

Problems of External Adaptation
* Consensus on the primary task, core mission, or manifest and latent functions of the group. * Consensus on goals, i.e. the concrete reflection of the core mission. * Consensus on the means to be used in accomplishing the goals. * Consensus on the criterion to be used in measuring how well the group is doing against its goals. * Consensus on remedial or repair strategies as needed when the group is not accomplishing its goals.
Problems of Internal Integration
* Common language and conceptual categories. * Consensus on group boundaries and criteria for inclusion and exclusion. * Consensus on criteria for the allocation of power and status. * Consensus on criteria for intimacy, friendship, and love. * Consensus on ideology.

[Schein, E.H., 1983, p.15]

Organizational culture is initially created by the founder(s) of a company. For example, the Watsons of IBM preached that their company was based on three corner-stones:

* "Respect for the individual" - Caring about the dignity and rights of each person in the organization, and not just when it is convenient or expedient to do so.

* "Customer service" - Giving the best customer service of any company in the world. Not some of the time, but all of the time.
* "Excellence" - Believing that all jobs should be performed in a superior way.

Similarly, Hewlett-Packard (HP), named after its two co-founders, has created a unique organizational culture as clearly spelt out in "The HP Way". The following concepts, expressed in the Way, teach its employees how the company works:

* Belief in people; freedom
* Respect and dignity; individual self-esteem
* Recognition; sense of achievement; participation
* Security; permanence; development of people
* Insurance; personal worry protection
* Sharing of benefits and responsibility
* Management by objectives (rather than directives)
* Informality; human relationships on a first-name basis; open communication
* Learning by making mistakes
* Performance and enthusiasm

Organizational culture is almost always created in the context of national culture. Yet many managers believe that organizational culture itself erases or at least diminishes the influence of national culture on corporate ideologies and organizational behaviors. They assume that, despite different cultural backgrounds, people working in the same organization become more similar than different. On the contrary, evidence suggests that far from reducing the influence, organizational culture in fact enhances national culture, in which the organization operates [31]. In other words, when placed within a foreign company, the local employees bring the values of their own national culture to the workplace and maintain or even strengthen their culturally specific way of working. For example, when working for a company from Japan, the Americans become more American, the Chinese more Chinese, and so on.

Our proposed model of comparative management (Figure 2-4) indicates that the values of organizational culture, usually expressed in corporate ideologies, affect management practices. The practices thus employed are then either reinforced or resisted by the values of national culture, as expressed in societal beliefs and attitudes. It may appear that the model points to a neat causal linkage between culture and management. However, one must be reminded that the main focus of our study here is on the management of an organization's social system, primarily human resource management, that is very much dependent on socio-cultural factors.

As a matter of fact, there is increasing evidence to support the contention that the overall management practices and effectiveness are as much, if not more, function of such contextual and environmental variables as size, technology, location, and economic, market and political conditions as they are of socio-cultural variables [32]. Negandhi, for one, has suggested a necessity for rethinking the issues by arguing against the cultural imperative hypothesis; it is also suggested that the patterns of relationships rather than the causal linkage be stressed in order to build and expand the knowledge of the functioning of complex organizations in different cultural settings [33]. Earlier on, we have simply stated that values are among the blocks of culture. But what is really culture? In order to better understand the patterns of relationship between culture and management, we need to get a firmer grip on the concept of culture itself.

CONCEPTS OF CULTURE

Culture is shared by a group of people, and exists in the minds of people. Culture is to a human collectivity what personality is to an individual. Culture determines the identity of a human group in the same way as personality determines the identity of an individual [34]. Culture is crystallized in the institutions people have built together such as family, education, religion, law, and literature; and it represents the national character [35]. Although these are some of the aspects of culture that make it significant to comparative management studies, the concept of culture itself is hard to define. It has been defined in so many different ways that no consensus has emerged.

Malinowski has stated that culture is a well-organized unity divided into two fundamental aspects - a body of artifacts (i.e. the tangible) and a system of customs (i.e. the intangible) [36]. Culture consists of the commodity and instruments as well as customs and bodily or mental habits of human needs. Similarly, Triandis and Lambert have described culture as the man-made part of the human environment including both physical objects (e.g. roads, buildings, tools) and subjective responses to what is man-made (e.g. myths, roles, values, attitudes) [37]. After cateloging more than 150 different definitions of culture, Kroeber and Kluckhorn offered one of the most comprehensive definitions [38]:

Culture consists of patterns, explicit and implicit of and for behavior acquired and transmitted by symbols, constituting the distinctive achievement of human groups, including their embodiment in artifacts; the essential core of culture consists of traditional (i.e. historically derived and selected) ideas and especially their attached values; cultural systems may, on the one hand, be considered as products of action, on the other as conditioning elements of future action.
[Kroeber, A.L. and C. Kluckhorn, 1952, p.181]

While culture is primarily born out of the satisfaction of biological needs by means of the commodity and instruments, its very nature makes man into something essentially different from other animals; man is also dependent on organized activities and cooperation to satisfy his psychological needs. Accordingly, culture must be understood from both tangible and intangible aspects. The nature of comparative management study dictates, however, that the intangible aspect should be emphasized. Keesing has identified four ways of thinking about the concept of culture [39]:

* Cultures as adaptive systems -- This approach assumes that cultures are systems of socially transmitted behavioral patterns that serve to relate human communities to their ecological settings; that cultural change is a process of adaptation; that adaptation is via economies and their social correlates, and also through ideational systems; that the ideational systems may strongly mediate cultural adaptation.
* Cultures as cognitive systems -- Culture is seen as being in the same realm as language, in other words as an inferred ideational code lying behind the realm of observable events.
* Cultures as structural systems -- This approach sees culture as cumulative creations of mind, and the results of the imposition by a group of patterned orders on the physical world.
* Cultures as symbolic systems -- In this approach, cultures are treated as systems of shared symbols and meanings, and are described in terms of humans engaging in symbolic action.

Searching for a concept of culture that provides for some tightening and improvements in its usefulness, Keesing has proposed that: culture is not all of what an individual knows, thinks, and feels about his world; it is his theory of what his fellows know, believe, and mean; it is an individual's theory of the code being followed, the game being played, in the society into which he was born; it is this theory to which a native actor refers. Keesing thus treats culture as the perceived rules of the game, but interacting with the game itself; the rules of the game change over time in accordance with the pattern of play and its results. In other words, culture changes over time. Such a change is often introduced to a society through its interaction with other societies.

CULTURE BEYOND NATIONAL BOUNDARIES

In world history, it has been an exception rather than a rule for a culture to spread over foreign countries slowly and in an atmosphere of peace and harmony. Typically, a sweeping assimilation of one culture into another is brought about and accompanied by military conquests. Almost always the conquerors impose their culture upon the conquered. However, there are always exceptions. The Japanese, for example, have been remarkably immune to the rule largely due to the fact that a foreign culture has never been forced on them by foreign invaders. As a result, they always felt that they could choose to accept or reject a foreign culture as they pleased [40]. Throughout their history, the Japanese only willingly borrowed foreign cultures that represented to them as something superior to their own.

In one way or another, cultures spread over countries. The word "culture" is usually reserved for countries, but it can be applied equally to ethnic or regional groups. Child and Kieser have pointed out that: culture may be defined as patterns of thoughts and manners which are widely shared; the boundaries of the social collectivity with which this sharing takes place are problematic so that it may make as much sense to refer to a class or regional culture as to a national culture [41].

A review of the literature shows that most cross-cultural research is actually cross-national studies, which means comparing not just culture but also socio-economic, political-legal, educational, and technological factors as well. Taking a view that the use of a national sample is not in the strictest sense a sample testing for the impact of culture, Kelley and Worthley conducted a study in order to isolate the role of culture and test its relationship to managerial attitudes [42]. They took samples of Japanese managers from Japan, and Japanese-American and Caucasian-American managers from Hawaii. Although their study indicated the importance of culture at least in terms of the formation of managerial attitudes, the statistical test supported much less fully the cultural differences between the two American groups than national ones between the Japanese group and the American group. The usefulness of their finding may be questioned in that the Japanese-American managers, most of whom are the second or even the third generation "Americans", are assumed to be still "Japanese" in the cultural sense.

Nevertheless, a study of this kind points out the importance of clearly defining the boundary of culture, when examining the transferability of management practices. Without a clear definition, we can hardly expect to make sense of comparative analysis of management across cultures.

It is, therefore, proposed that we define culture as the interactive aggregate of common characteristics that influence a human group's response to its environment. We have, in effect, adopted Keesing's concept, that treats culture as the perceived rules of the game being played in a society [43]. Such rules interact with the game itself; they change over time in accordance with the patterns of play and its results. And the rules of the game are generated by the values commonly found in a society within and even beyond its national boundary.

Equipped with this definition of culture, we can now begin investigations on an issue that has received very little attention to date in the comparative management circle - the transferability of Japanese-style management practices across East Asian cultures. Our study thus aims at moving forward Comparative Management Theory on the basis of data from East Asian, rather than Euro-American, cultures. It represents an Asian initiative in comparative management research which has long been dominated by the Western initiatives. To get started, we first need to know more about the Japanese-style management itself. And this will be the topic to be dealt with in the next chapter.

NOTES

1. Adler, N.J., _International Dimensions of Organization Behavior_, Boston: Kent Publishing Co., (1986)

2. Schollhammer, H., "The Comparative Management Jungle" in Farmer, R.N., R.W. Stevens, and H. Schollhammer (eds.), _Readings in International Business_, Encino, Calif.: Dickenson Publishing Co., (1972)

3. Negandhi, A.R., "Three Decades of Cross-Cultural Management Research: Alice in Wonderland" in Clegg, S.R., D.C. Dunphy and S.G. Redding (eds.), Enterprise and Management in East Asia, Hong Kong: Center of Asian Studies, (1986), pp.35-36

4. Roberts, K.H., "On Looking at an Elephant: An Evaluation of Cross-Cultural Research Related to Organizations" in Weinshall, T.D. (ed.), Culture and Management, Middlesex: Penguin Books, (1977), pp.56-104

5. Newman, W.H., "Comparative Management: A Resource for Improving Managerial Adaptability", Columbia Journal of World Business, (Summer 1978), pp.5-6

6. Harbison, H. and C. Myers, Management in the Industrial World, New York: McGraw-Hill, (1959)

7. Koontz, H., and C. O'Donnell, Principles of Management, New York: McGraw-Hill, (1968)

8. Adler, N.J., "Cross-Cultural Management Research: Ostrich and the Trend", Academy of Management Review, (April 1983), pp.226-232

9. Oberg, W., "Cross-Cultural Perspective on Management Principles", Academy of Management Journal, (June 1963), pp.129-143

10. Bedeian, A., "A Comparison and Analysis of German and United States Managerial Attitudes toward the Legitimacy of Organizational Influence", Academy of Management Journal, (1975), vol.18, pp.897-904

11. Farmer, R.N. and B.M. Richman, "A Model for Research in Comparative Management", California Management Review, (Winter 1964), pp.55-68

12. Schollhammer, H., (1972), op.cit.

13. Negandhi, A.R. and B.D. Estafen, "A Research Model to Determine the Applicability of American Management Knowhow in Differing Cultures and/or Environments", Academy of Management Journal, (Dec. 1965), pp.309-318

14. Haire, M., E. Ghiselli and L. Porter, Managerial Thinking: An International Study, New York: John Wiley & Sons, (1966)

15. Hofstede, G., Culture's Consequences: International Differences in Work-Related Values, Beverly Hills, Calif.: Sage Publications, (1984)

16. Gennaro, F.D., "International Transfer of Management Skills: The Behavioral Patterns - A Preliminary Study", The Quarterly Journal of AIESEC International, (Jan.-Mar. 1969), pp.30-48

17. Negandhi, A.R., (1986), op.cit.

18. Roberts, K.H., (1977), op.cit.

19. Davis, S.M., Comparative Management: Organizational and Cultural Perspective, Englewood Cliffs: Prentice-Hall, (1971)

20. Adler, N.J., (1986), op.cit.

21. Abegglen, J.C., The Japanese Factory: Aspects of its Social Organization, Glencoe, Ill.: The Free Press, (1958)

22. Dore, R.P., British Factory, Japanese Factory: The Origins of National Diversity in Industrial Relations, London: George Allen & Unwin, (1973)

23. Peterson, R.B., "Future Directions in Comparative Management Research: Where we have been and where we should be going", International Management Newsletter, (Fall 1986), pp.5-10

24. Negandhi, A.R. and B.D. Estafen, (1965), op.cit.

25. Schollhammer, H., (1972), op.cit.

26. Estafen, B.D., "An Empirical Experiment in Comparative Management: A Study of the Transferability of American Management Policies and Practices into Chile", Ph.D. thesis, Los Angeles: University of California, (1967)

27. Negandhi, A.R., "Transfer of Advanced Management Practices and Knowhow into the Industrial Enterprises in Taiwan: An Empirical Finding", Soochow Journal of Literature and Social Studies, (September 1971), p.35-54

28. Parsons, T., "Suggestions for Sociological Approach to the Theory of Organizations", Administrative Science Quarterly, (June 1956), pp.62-85

29. Negandhi, A.R., (1986), op.cit.

30. Schein, E.H., "The Role of the Founder in Creating Organizational Culture", Organizational Dynamics, (Summer 1983), pp.13-28

31. Adler, N.F., (1986), op.cit.

32. Child, J., "Culture, Contingency and Capitalism in the Cross-National Study of Organizations" in Cummings, L.L. and B.M. Shaw (eds.), Research in Organizational Behavior, Vol. III, Greenwich, CT: JAI Press, (1981)

33. Negandhi, A.R., (1986), op.cit.

34. Hofstede, G., (1984), op.cit.

35. Shermerhorn, J.R., Jr., Management for Productivity, New York: John Wiley & Sons, (1986)

36. Malinowski, B., A Scientific Theory of Culture and Other Essays, Chapel Hill: University of North Carolina Press, (1944)

37. Triandis, H.C. and W.W. Lambert, Handbook of Cross-Cultural Psychology, Boston: Allyn & Bacon, (1980)

38. Kroeber, A.L. and C. Kluckhorn, "Culture: A Critical Review of Concepts and Definitions", Cambridge, MA: Peabody Museum Papers, (1952), vol.47, no.1

39. Keesing, R.M., "Theories of Culture", Annual Review of Anthropology, (1974)

40. Ozaki, R.S., The Japanese: A Cultural Portrait, Rutland, VT: Charles E. Tuttle, (1979)

41. Child, J. and A. Kieser, "A Contrast in British and West German Management Practices: Are Recipes for Success Culture-bound?", paper presented at the Conference on Cross-Cultural Studies on Organizational Functioning, Hawaii, (1977)

42. Kelley, L. and R. Worthley, "The Role of Culture in Comparative Management: a Cross-Cultural Perspective", Academy of Management Journal, (March 1981), pp.164-173

43. Keesing, R.M., (1974), op.cit.

Chapter Three

THE MODELS OF JAPANESE MANAGEMENT: HOW DISTINCTIVE ARE THEY?

Since the end of the World War II, the vast majority of Japanese authorities on management have been under strong influence of the Western management theories. As a result, there have been very few researchers in Japan who have tried to analyze and theorize the realities of Japanese-style management. However, there are indigenous practices in Japan to contrast with those in the West. In the absence of clearly formulated theories of management in Japan, therefore, we must resort to the studies of Japanese-style management practices, which have been conducted extensively over the last few years, in order to understand the indigenousness of Japanese management. In this chapter, we shall first trace the evolution of management theories that have taken place in the West since the turn of this century, and then go on to examine several models of Japanese management that have been built upon the facts - the practices employed to manage ideas, things, and people. By doing so, it is hoped that we could see how the Japanese have managed to develop their unique features of management while borrowing very heavily the concepts of management from the West.

EXPLANATION OF MANAGEMENT

"What is management?" This is a simple question. Yet there is no simple answer. Despite its crucial importance and high visibility, management remains as the least understood of our basic institutions. The difficulty to explain management is in part due to the fact that the study of management as a separate academic discipline did not take root until the turn of this century. There are basically two ways to explain what management is: (a) deductive form of

47

explanation - deducing the particular from the general, and (b) inductive form of explanation - inducing the general from the particular.

Those who take the first form of explanation maintain that "management does not really exist; it is a word, an idea, and abstraction" [1]. They attempt to explain management by subsuming the puzzling particulars under general propositions. In other words, they start the study of management from a theory. Theory then offers a conceptual scheme by which the relevant phenomena are systematized, classified, and interrelated; it predicts facts [2]. The main interest here is to determine conceptually what managers ought to do.

In contrast to this theory-oriented approach, those who take the second form of explanation argue that management is practiced by human beings who really exist and, therefore, it is not an abstraction. Accordingly, they start the study of management from facts. In his widely-read book "The Practice of Management", first published in 1954, Peter Drucker stated that management could only be explained by analyzing functions that managers actually performed [3]. Mintzberg also maintains that it is not admissible to spin out the fact-free theory of management from the cozy depth of an armchair [4]. In other words, they believe that one cannot bask in the warm sunshine of a theory before one has plunged into the cold water of facts, which can only be obtained through systematic studies of managerial work.

The theory-fact dichotomy seems to suggest a division between the theorists, who assert the priority of imaginative theory over facts, and the fact-finders, who assert the priority of facts over theory. However, as shown in Figure 3-1, these two seemingly contrasting approaches are not necessarily mutually exclusive but complementary to each other. After all, regardless of the starting point, both aim at developing a useful tool that will help lift research progressively to a new relevant stage of work and spotlight major problems involved in the undertaking.

Figure 3-1: The Development of Management Theory

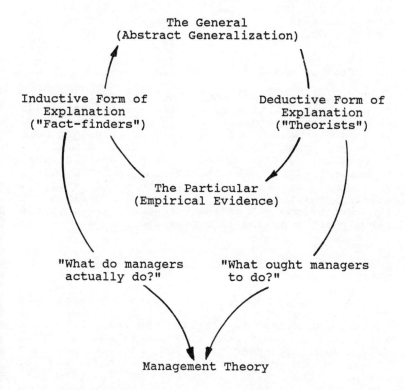

Management can be regarded as a science (i.e. organized knowledge), which consists of four distinct operations [5]:

* Conceptualization and classification
* Theory testing
* Systematic empirical observation
* Theory discovery

The theory-oriented approach is critical for the first two operations, and the fact-oriented approach for the last two operations. We have available today the knowledge needed for the successful practice of management. Knowledge is organized around theory (i.e. a structure of fundamental concepts and principles); it must be applied to practice effectively and artfully in a given situation. Yet there still exists the gap between the knowledge and actual practice of management. We, therefore, need to narrow the gap by gaining a further understanding on what managers ought to do as well as what managers actually do.

EVOLUTION OF MANAGEMENT THEORIES

Although it was not until the very early part of this century that a systematic body of knowledge related to management began to be developed, various schools of management thought have rapidly sprung up since. This led to confusion, contradiction, and controversy as to what management is. The "Management Theory Jungle", as coined by Koontz back in the early 1960s, is still luxuriant [6]. Let us now briefly trace the evolution of management theories that has taken place over the last nine decades.

Scientific Management Movement and Classical Schools

In the early 1900s, the scientific management movement came to surface under the driving force of an American industrial engineer Frederick Taylor, who is widely regarded as the Father of Scientific Management. The movement focused primarily on developing the one best way to perform the task in order to increase the productive efficiency of workers based on scientific methods and techniques. Its emphasis was on making management a science rather than an art, thus signalling a clean break from the past tradition in the study of management. The fundamental principles that Taylor saw underlying the scientific approach to management may be summarized as follows [7]:

* Replace rules of thumb with science
* Obtain harmony in group action, rather than discord
* Achieve cooperation of human-beings, rather than chaotic individualism
* Work for maximum output, rather than restricted output

* Develop all workers to the fullest extent possible for their own and their company's highest prosperity

Some of the techniques (e.g. time-and-motion studies) that he and his followers developed to put these principles into practice had certain mechanistic aspects. However, contrary to the popular belief, throughout Taylor's written work runs a strong humanistic theme as well.

Scientific management was concerned with optimizing work efforts at the operational level. However, during the first half of the 20th century, there developed a theory whose primary focus was to establish general principles applicable to higher levels. Henri Fayol - a leading French industrialist at the time - who developed a comprehensive list of principles is generally considered as the Father of Management Theory. His principles are:

* Specialization of labor
* Clear definition of authority and responsibility
* Order and discipline in the workplace
* Scalar chain and unity of command and direction
* Equity and the fair remuneration of personnel
* Stability of the tenure of personnel
* Initiative at all levels of organizational ladder
* Spirit of cooperation

Fayol and his followers, who had established the Management Process School, advocate that management is a universal process that can be defined in terms of five functions that the manager performs, i.e. planning, organizing, staffing, directing, and controlling. However, it should be emphasized that Fayol himself recognized that the principles of management listed above were neither absolute nor rigid. He explained: "principles are flexible and capable of adaptation to every need; it is a matter of knowing how to make use of them." [8]

Another major pillar in the development of classical management theory was provided by the German sociologist Max Weber, who had developed the Theory of Bureaucracy. The concept of bureaucracy herein connotes neither good nor bad in terms of performance but rather refers to certain characteristics of organizational design. Weber viewed bureaucracy as the best form that could be used most effectively for large and complex organizations, arising from the needs of modern society. The basic concepts of bureaucracy include [9]:

* A division of labor based on fuctional specialization
* A well-defined hierarchy of authority
* A system of rules covering the rights and duties of positional incumbents
* A system of procedures for dealing with work situations
* Impersonality of interpersonal relations
* Promotion and selection for employment based on technical competence

Following the initial development of these classical management theories, several new forces from both within and outside the organization had driven forth the evolution of management theory. The major forces came from two different directions - management sciences and behavioral sciences.

Management Sciences and Behavioral Sciences

Management Sciences (MS), sometimes referred to as Operations Research (OR) or more broadly as MS/OR, is a natural extension of the earlier scientific management movement. Under the scientific movement, it was the industrial engineers and practicing managers who had applied scientific methods and techniques to operational problem solving. By contrast, in management sciences, the scientists, gathered from different disciplines, contributed their respective expert knowledge to managerial problem solving. Although management sciences are a rather loose conglomeration of interests and approaches, there are key concepts that permeate the field:

* Emphasis on scientific method
* Systematic approach to problem solving
* Mathematical model building
* Orientation to normative rather than descriptive models
* Emphasis on economic and technical aspects
* Rational decision-making under uncertainty

The management scientists such as the Nobel-prize winner Herbert Simon - a founder of the Decision Theory School - take a view that the manager is a decision-maker who uses systematic analysis and quantitative techniques to optimize performance toward the organization's overall objectives.

On the other hand, the behavioral scientists made an attempt to put the human elements back into organizations - the aspect that they felt that the classical theorists had minimized. The earlier behavioral scientists, perhaps as best represented by Elton Mayo, thus stressed the psychological and social aspects of organization and management, rather than economic and technical aspects, as the important factors that would determine worker satisfaction and productivity. They developed many concepts about human behavior in organizations, which included:

* The individual is motivated not only by economic incentives but also by diverse social and psychological factors.
* The informal work group has an important role in determining the attitudes and performance of individual workers.
* Democratic rather than authoritarian leadership patterns should be emphasized.
* Increased worker satisfaction will lead to higher productivity.
* Effective communication is essential for worker participation in decision-making and management functions.
* Management requires effective social skills as well as technical skills.

Mayo's followers such as Douglas McGregar, Frederick Herzberg, and Abraham Maslow have developed some of the most profound Theories of Motivation to explain why people behave in the ways they do and what managers can do to encourage certain types of behavior while discouraging others. Their work will be discussed in some detail later in Chapter Seven.

Contemporary Schools of Management Thought

The theory and practice of management go hand-in-hand, and they have naturally evolved together over the years. As can be seen in Figure 3-2, the start of rapid development of management theories coincided with significant changes in the practice of management at the turn of this century - from a highly individualistic approach to less individualistic and more scientific approach to management. Management then began to be treated not merely as an art but also as a science, thus decreasing its reliance on the rules of thumb, personal judgement, intuition, experience etc. and increasing reliance on the scientific methods and techniques. Though most people today agree that theories are an important tool of management, there is a controversy over which theory is really the best.

In recent years, there developed one overriding approach to the study of management - the Systems Approach. Underlying this approach is a concept that the organization is a system of mutually dependent parts and variables; and management is viewed as an important component of the organization system, whose function is to coordinate and interrelate the activities and achieve the objectives of the entire system. This is not an entirely new concept. The treatment of the organization as a social system was advocated as early as in the 1930s by Chester Barnard who wrote one of the most influential books on management - "The Functions of the Executive" - during his tenure as the president of the New Jersey Bell Telephone Co. In the book, he remarked that the most useful concept for the analysis of experience of cooperative systems was embodied in the definition of a formal organization as a system of consciously coordinated activities or forces of two or more persons [10].

The systems concept views the organization as a system which exhibits very complex relationships not only internally but also with its external environment. It has in fact provided a basic framework for the subsequent development of Situational or Contingency Theory of Management that is directed toward suggesting appropriate managerial actions contingent upon specific conditions. Burns and Stalker's study is significant for having thrown light on how organizations must vary if they are to cope effectively with different environmental conditions [11]. In essence, their study suggested that there are two divergent systems of management practice - a mechanistic system that

Figure 3-2: Evolution of Management Theories

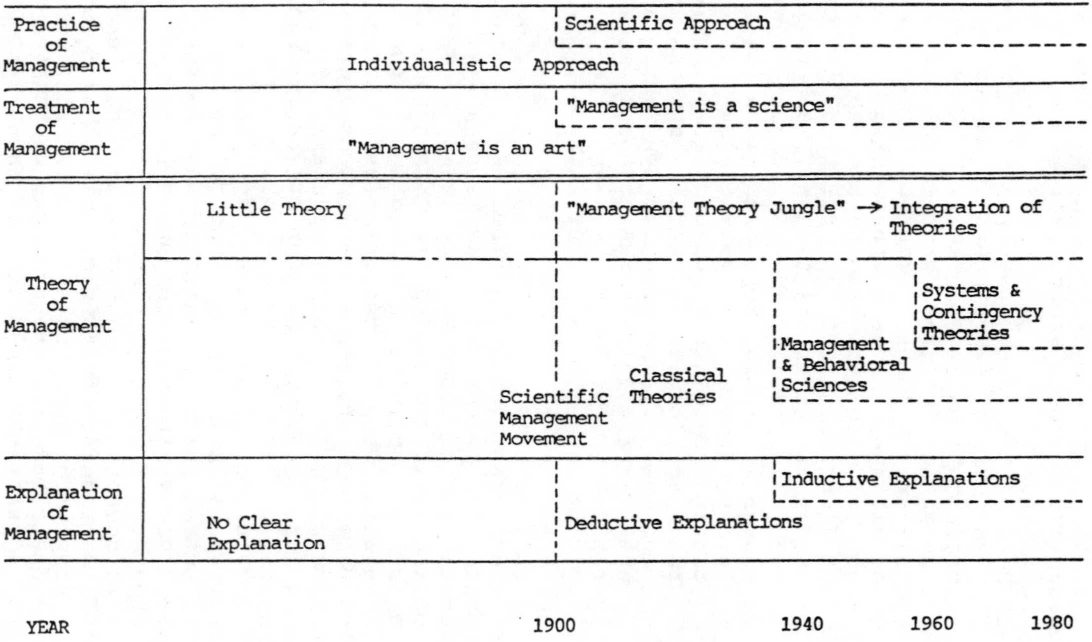

			Scientific Approach	
Practice of Management		Individualistic Approach		
Treatment of Management			"Management is a science"	
		"Management is an art"		
Theory of Management	Little Theory		"Management Theory Jungle" → Integration of Theories	Systems & Contingency Theories
				Management & Behavioral Sciences
		Scientific Management Movement	Classical Theories	
Explanation of Management	No Clear Explanation		Deductive Explanations	Inductive Explanations
YEAR	1900		1940	1960 1980

is appropriate to an enterprise operating under relatively stable conditions, and an organic system which is required for conditions of change. Also in the book published in 1970, Lorsch and Lawrence wrote [12]:

> During the past few years, there has been evident a new trend in the study of organizational phenomena... Rather than searching for the panacea of the one best way to organize under all conditions, investigators have more and more tended to examine the functioning of organizations in relation to the needs of their particular members and the external pressures facing them. Basically, this approach seems to be leading to the development of a Contingency Theory of organization with the appropriate internal states and processes of the organization contingent upon external requirements and member needs.
> [Lorsch, J.W. and P.R. Lawrence, 1970, p.1]

The Systems and Contingency Theories do not provide the general principles of management applicable to all organizations and situations. However, the concept underlying the systems and contingency approaches to management analysis could well provide a basis for reconciling and integrating the diverse theories with the premise that all theories are not competitive but compatible [13]. Since the early 1960s when we were in the thick Management Theory Jungle, the vegetation in the jungle has changed somewhat. New approaches have been developed and older approaches have taken on some new meanings, but the development of management theory still has the characteristics of a jungle [14].

MODELS OF JAPANESE MANAGEMENT

As described in the previous section, the birth and subsequent evolution of management theories took place in the West. And no indigenous theory of management has ever been clearly formulated in Japan, but there are indigenous Japanese practices to contrast with those in the West. In recent years, they have been studied extensively both within and outside Japan largely due to increased interest to uncover reasons for Japan's rapid rise to join the ranks of economic superpowers. Findings from numerous comparative studies of Japanese and Western managements should, therefore, help us build the models that could explain what Japanese management is.

Based on his observations as an American executive working for a major advertising agency in Japan, Yang has described Japanese management as an organic type and American management as a system type [15]. Table 3-1 presents a summary of the comparative characteristics of organic and system types of management. Under the system type of management, the top executive is a designer of the management system, a strategic planner, and a decision-maker all in one; he sees himself as a professional manager. By contrast, under the organic type of management, the top executive is a facilitator, who creates a favorable climate in which the company operates; he sees his main role as that of a social leader.

Table 3-1: Characteristics of Management
-- Japan versus the US

Japan ("organic" type)	US ("system" type)
Facilitator	Decision-maker
Social leader	Professional
Group strength	Individual initiative and creativity
Free-form command	Hierarchical command
Emphasis on human relations	Emphasis on functional relationships
Management by consensus	Management by objectives

The strength of the system type of management lies in the individual initiative and creativity. On the other hand, a strong collectivity orientation and a high degree of emotional commitment of individual members to the group constitute one of the notable strengths of the organic type of management. The system type of management places great emphasis on functional relationships between subsystems within an organization, and it generally works through a hierarchical chain of command to achieve the integration of subsystems into a total system. By comparison, the organic type of management places its emphasis on human relations and tends to prefer a free-form command. In resolving conflicts among dissident individuals, the system type normally finds it effective to rely on "Management by Objectives" technique. Under the organic type of management, however, the top executive relies on "Management by Consensus" technique, and he often plays a crucial role in bringing about a consensus.

In summary, as shown in Figure 3-3, the organic type of Japanese management relies on group strength in order to deal with internal and external adversaries. It places heavy emphasis on human relations, generally resulting in highly effective human resource management. However, the decision-making process is so cumbersome that small decisions, even when obviously needed, are very often not made at all. The absence of clearly-formulated plans, particularly those of a strategic nature could, therefore, lead to ineffective long-range planning, at least in the Western sense. By contrast, the system type of American management relies on individual strength in dealing with various adversaries. It places great emphasis on functional relationships, rather than human relations, generally resulting in effective long-range planning but relatively ineffective human resource management.

Figure 3-3: Relative Strength, Emphasis, and
          Effectiveness of Management --
          Japanese versus American

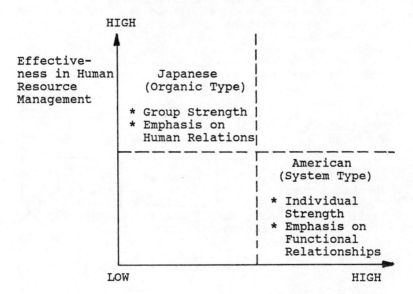

Figure 3-4 is an abbreviated illustration of management process as described by MacKenzie [16]. Although it largely presents the view of the classical school of management thought, it could be a useful framework for our analysis of Japanese management practices. Figure 3-4 indicates that the manager basically manages three elements - "ideas", "things", and "people". The elements are reflected in three main tasks accomplished by the manager:

* Conceptual thinking -- The formulation of new
         business ideas and opportunities to set
         the organizational objectives.

* Administration -- The coordination of material and other organizational resources within the formal structure.
* Leadership -- The recruitment, guidance, and motivation of people to achieve the organizational objectives.

Figure 3-4: Elements, Tasks, and Functions of Management

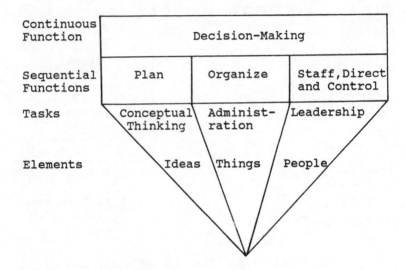

Whereas the five functions from planning through controlling are, to a large extent, performed sequentially, decision-making occurs repeatedly and continuously throughout the management process. As noted earlier, the Japanese management typically shows relatively low effectiveness in long-range planning (i.e. the management of ideas) but high effectiveness in human resource management (i.e. the management of people). In the following sections, we shall further analyze the Japanese practices by examining the management of these two elements as well as things in Japan.

The Management of Ideas

Planning is usually considered as the most basic
of all functions performed by the manager. Not
only is planning a basic function for all
managers at all levels in the enterprise, but
also the four other functions of the manager must
reflect it. Thus, a manager organizes, staffs,
directs and leads, and controls to assure the
attainment of goals according to plans [17].
Planning could be viewed as a rational decision-
making endeavor to set and achieve a feasible
objective most efficiently. Here, the underlying
premises of corporate planning are largely of
Western origin. The four main ingredients in the
corporate planning process and their associated
premises are shown in Table 3-2.

Table 3-2: The Premises of Western Corporate
Planning

Ingredient in Corporate Planning Process	Associated Premise
Information	Active, structured, and systematic mode of environmental monitoring
Objective	Careful feasibility assessment in objective-setting
Means	Formulation and adjustment of specified programs for action (i.e. plans) based on an overall framework designated to create maximum consistency in chrono-logical and fuctional dimensions
Implementation	Close monitoring of plans for effective implementation, per-formance evaluation, and feedback

Many writers have noted that the Japanese
practices in respect to planning significantly

deviate from the Western premises. In fact, the Japanese practices appear to be just the opposite in all important aspects. Kono, for example, attributed such a contrast to the perceived purpose of corporate planning [18]. In the West, long-range planning is generally used to make strategic decisions based on a set of clearly-defined objectives, the highest of which are determined by the top executive himself. However, in Japan, it is simply used to clarify goals and policies of the company. Hayashi has also noted that the primary purpose of corporate planning in Japan is not to formulate strategic programs for action and to implement them. Instead, it is primarily to set up targets of endeavor and draw the future portrait of the company, to unify managerial thoughts within the company, and to create an achievement orientation and motivational effect in the company [19].

The Japanese social psychologist Yoshikawa has observed that a Western concept like Management by Objectives (MBO) is frowned upon by Japanese managers; as a result, detailed and specific long-range plans are not generally considered viable [20]. Obviously, in the absence of well-formulated long-range plans, it is not possible to install an effective control mechanism for performance evaluation, in the Western sense.

Since its advent, first put together by Peter Drucker back in the mid-1950s [21], the concept of MBO has attracted much attention and interest from business and academic circles. To a great extent, MBO has been adopted by many progressive companies in the US and other Western countries. Yet more than thirty years later, there remains much doubt and debate about its effectiveness. MBO, by definition, places its core issue on participation - all employees are to be actively involved in the entire process of management, beginning with planning and ending with control. However, in most instances, the manager, under the disguised participation, still exercises authoritarian leadership, gives out goals and objectives to his subordinates through a one-way channel of communication, and leaves little room to the subordinates for decision-making.

There is strong evidence for the need to change the very concept of participation [22]. It calls for a shift from "boss-oriened" MBO to "employee-centered" MBO, as reflected in democratic leadership style, two-way channel of communication and, especially, employees' active role in decision-making. Perhaps, we could say that Japanese managers have been actually practicing the employee-centered MBO for many years. This may be best illustrated by Japanese-style decision-making.

In examining the planning function of management so far, w have adopted a classical view that describes the manager as a reflective, systematic planner. However, there are criticisms to such a view. Mintzberg, for example, has noted that when we watch what managers really do, we cannot always relate what we see to planning or any other functions [23]. The evidence suggests that managers work at an unrelenting pace, that their activities are characterized by brevity, variety, and discontinuity, and that they are strongly oriented to action and dislike reflective activities. Nevertheless, he has pointed out that there is one common role that all managers play - decision-making. In fact, decision-making is considered synonymous with management by many scholars, who believe that decision-making and the process leading to it account for most of what managers actually do. Simon is probably responsible more than any other individual for developing a modern decision theory. He describes that the decision-making process in its broadest context is composed of three major phases: Intelligence, Design, and Choice [24]. The process can actually be divided into five steps:

1) Definition of problems and opportunities
2) Analysis of problems and opportunities
3) Generation of alternative courses of action
4) Selection of an optimum course of action
5) Implementation of the choice

It is generally agreed in the West that the top management plays a very active role from step-1 through step-4 in making an important decision of strategic nature, which will then be communicated down progressively to the lower levels for implementation. The decision-making process commonly adopted in Japan is basically the same as the Western one. However, the role of the top management is, in large part, limited to the initial definition of problems and opportunities and, to a lesser extent, the selection of a best possible course of action. Hattorri has noted [25]:

> As far as the top management is concerned the way the problem is recognized and presented to the middle managers for analysis and resolution really determines the quality of the decision-making ... and it is difficult for the top executive to reject proposals worked out ... as a result of the combined efforts of many people.
>
> [Hattorri, I., 1978, p.13]

Figure 3-5 shows a modified model of the Japanese system of decision-making, commonly known as the "ringi" system, as suggested by Hattorri.

Figure 3-5: "Ringi" System of Decision-Making

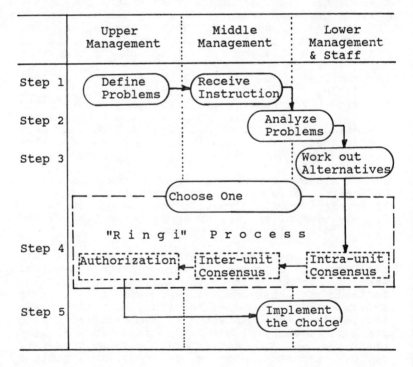

Figure 3-6: A Sample "Ringi-sho"

						urgent

(Titles & Seals of the Top Executives)

(Titles & Seals of Proposers)

| | Approval No.: |
| Proposal Date: |
| Approval Date: |

Conditions for approval:

| *Subject: Additional Fund for Advertising Campaign | *Origin of Proposal Overseas Operation Division |

| *Budget: U.S.$500,000.- | Account No. | | | | | |

*Summary of Proposal:

Our North American subsidiary has a goal of achieving the sales of $45 million for next year as compared with $40 million for this year.

In the light of mounting competition in the market, it is of the utmost importance to improve our product image through a more aggressive advertising campaign.

Accordingly, we wish to have your authorization for additional fund to carry out the campaign, with the budgetary ceiling of $500,00.

Opinions:

| *Documents Attached: | Received | Date: handling no: |

ᒪ— (Seals of Handlers)

* To be filled by proposers

The "ringi" system of decision-making was first explained as one of the most important features of Japanese management by a group of Japan's management scholars during their fact-finding mission to the US in the late 1950s. What makes this model so distinct from the Western model is the inclusion of the "ringi" process, used for the selection of one best solution, as a component of the total system of decision-making. "Rin" means submitting a proposal to one's superior and receiving his approval. "Gi" means deliberation and decisions. This is a process whereby a proposal, the "ringi-sho" (see Figure 3-6: A Sample "Ringi-sho") is prepared at the lower level of management and circulated to all affected units for review, revision, or approval.

It is important to note that the "ringi" process is almost always preceded by what the Japanese call "nemawashi" - informal discussion and consultation before the formal proposal is presented. It may be regarded as a means of horizontal communication to supplement vertical communication within the organization. In American or European organizations, people work in private or partitioned rooms, and the communication channels and the direction of information flow are clearly defined. In this setup, the top management is at the center of the communication channels and serves as the central figure in the decision-making process. By contrast, in Japanese organizations, people normally work together in a big room, and the communication channels take a form of network resembling a fishing net. Each individual thus creates his own communication network and serves as the central figure in the decision-making process within the fishing net.

"Nemawashi" is actually a horticultural term, which refers to the cutting of roots and rotation of the trunk of a tree to free it for transplantation. This is considered as an important step, where the greatest care is required to ensure a subsequent success in moving a tree from one location to another. It is a process very similar in spirit to informal talks preceding the formal submission and circulation of a proposal. The abrupt submission of a proposal without "nemawashi" is seen as a lack of sensitivity contrary to the Japanese spirit, which reveres the preservation of a harmonious atmosphere within the organization.

The "ringi" process is characterized by its bottom-up approach and collective decision-making by consensus. It must, however, be noted that the "ringi" process alone does not constitute the total system of decision-making. It is just one component of the total system. In fact, the important parts of decision-making, including the problem definition and analysis, are performed prior to this particular step, following the top-down approach. Therefore, the "ringi" system of decision-making should not simply be equated with the bottom-up approach; it actually adopts both top-down and bottom-up approaches.

It is not uncommon for the "ringi-sho" to be merely the formalization of a decision from the top management which has had the benefits of prior discussion before being drafted. Considerable discretion is still retained by individual managers to prescribe in detail when and by whom a decision will be made and implemented. Contrary to a popular belief about collective decision-making in Japan, the ultimate responsibility for all decisions still rests, in large part, with the top executive. Given an organizational climate which encourages harmony and discourages criticisms, it may be more accurate to label the Japanese system of decision-making as a system of "Decision-making by Consensual Understanding" rather than simply as that of "Decision-making by Consensus" [26].

The Management of Things

To a significant degree, the concept of duties and responsibilities that the management holds determines the way in which the organization is structured. American management tends to place heavy emphasis on functional relationships, whereby each individual is expected to perform a specific function and conscious efforts are made to clearly demarcate the individual's duty. Under this type of management, priority is placed on each individual performing a job assigned to him. As a result, the job, for which his responsibility is also expressly defined, becomes the basic unit in structuring the organization.

Japanese management, on the other hand, fosters group strength and places more emphasis on human relations within and among groups than on functional relationships. The duty assigned to a particular individual is not always clearly defined, and priority is put on accomplishing tasks given out to groups - section, department, division, and other units of the workforce. As a result, a task, for which the individual responsibility is only vaguely defined, is accomplished by the individual's strong sense of responsibility toward the group. A task thus becomes the basic unit in structuring the organization.

The Japanese, on the whole, carry out the group tasks based on the unwritten rules of situational conformity, i.e. the sharp perception of the situation and the unique balance with reality, and the quick orientation and reaction to cope with various situations [27]. The Japanese worker quickly reads the circumstances he is placed in (e.g. his own and surrounding situations, his colleagues's reactions) and tries to respond to the needs arising from the overall situation. As a result, in Japan, the manager does not have to spell out to his subordinates exactly what to do or how to do it.

For example, when he must be away from the office for hours or even days, all that he would have to do is to simply say, "Do as you think fit." This is well reflected in the free form of command generally used in the Japanese organization. The same may not apply in the US. Japanese managers who have spent a few years in the US often comment that if they do not give specific instructions to American workers, they would be bombarded with questions like "What am I supposed to do?", "How should I do this?", or "Why do I have to do this?"

Generally speaking, when compared with their Japanese counterparts, American workers lack situational conformity in performing jobs at the workplace. This could explain why the hierarchical command, rather than the free-form command, is used in American organizations. Iwata has compared Japanese and American organizations by describing the former as the Human Co-working Model and the latter as the Machine Model [28]:

> Whereas an American or European organization is like a precision machine made up of a combination of parts that do not have self-mobility capabilities, a Japanese organization is like an organism that consists of cells (e.g. sections and departments), that cannot exist independently but do act on their own to some extent in accordance with the situations that come up.
>
> [Iwata, R., 1982, p.68]

Similarly, Campbell's comparative analysis of the meaning of work has suggested that the American approach is basically mechanistic, whereas the Japanese approach is organic [29]. The Americans tend to focus on understanding the meaning of work in terms of a "job-worker" fit. In this approach, a job is assigned to a suitable worker. By contrast, the Japanese shift the focus from the nature of the job to the nature of the worker (i.e."worker-job" fit) - a worker is assigned to a suitable job. In the organic approach adopted by the Japanese, an individual is seen as being able and willing to recognize the critical role he plays and ultimately determines the meaning of work himself. This may explain why Japanese workers expend relatively more energy on their organizational tasks, following the unwritten rules of situational conformity.

Morita, the head of SONY and one of Japan's internationally best-known business executives, has referred to American organizations as being like brick walls while Japanese organizations are more like stone walls [30]:

> In an American company, the company's plans are all made up in advance, and the framework for each job is decided upon. Then, the company sets out to find a person to fit each job ... so this structure is like a wall built of bricks; the shape of each employee must fit in perfectly, or not at all. In Japan, recruits are hired, and then we (managers) have to learn how to make use of them. They are a highly educated but irregular lot. The manager takes a good long look at these rough stones, and he has to build a wall by combining them in the best possible way ... Japanese managers must also think of the shapes of these stones as changing from time to time. As the business changes, it becomes necessary to refit stones into different places.
>
> [Morita, A., 1987, p.190]

Figure 3-7 shows the contrasting concepts of duties and responsibilities in Japanese and American organizations, which could have important implications for the organizational structure. In the diagram, the white area represents individuals, while the shaded area belongs to a group. In a typical Japanese company, the group area, where any particular individual's duties and responsibilities are ambiguous, is consciously kept large. Each individual in the group is thus expected to expand or shrink his own area, depending on circumstances (e.g. his own and colleagues' ability or amount of work). In other words, there are no rigid lines showing where his duties and responsibilities end, and individuals remain very flexible in this respect. In contrast to this, in a typical American company, the organization is rigidly structured; and each individual is placed within the confines of his own duties and responsibilities. The area belonging to the group is, therefore, kept to a minimum.

Figure 3-7: Concepts of Duty and Responsibility

A Work-Unit in Japan   A Work-Unit in the US

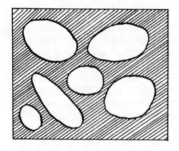
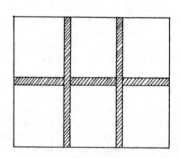

In the US, individual members comprising various parts of the group tend to be considered replaceable. If a vacancy arises, it is quickly filled by someone, usually recruited from the external labor market. By contrast, the members of the group in a Japanese organization are not considered replaceable parts that merely perform assigned jobs. Instead, every individual is regarded as an indispensable member of the group. If anyone leaves the group (or is absent from work), someone within the group immediately steps in to fill the gap by expanding his area of duties and responsibilities. The American concept of duty and responsibility, as embodied in job-specifications and work-manuals, has not taken root in Japanese organizations.

The Management of People

Our examination of the management of ideas and things (i.e. planning and organizing functions) so far has already revealed a number of features that make Japanese management quite distinct from Western management. Table 3-3 shows the main features of Japanese management that are most frequently cited by the observers of Japanese business organizations. The first two can be considered as the ideologies of Japanese management; the rest are those related to practices which are affected by the ideologies. Taken together, these features characterize Japanese-style management, whose effectiveness is often used to explain high work motivation and productivity in Japan. Let us now examine the third and last element of management - people (i.e. Human Resource Management or HRM) - in order to further our understanding of Japanese-style management.

A survey conducted recently in Japan has shown that the goup-oriented ideology of Japanese management is still prevalent [31]. Seventy-five per cent of the companies surveyed said that the interests of a group should be placed over those of an individual, against 24 per cent who said that they should not. Community-oriented ideology was also confirmed by the survey. When asked whether the company should concern itself with the private life of its employees, 61 per cent said yes, while 37 per cent disagreed. Figure 3-8 is an abbreviated model of Japanese-style HRM proposed by Ishida [32].

Based on the ideologies that emphasize group and community orientations, Japanese firms typically adopt a strategy for internalizing the labor market. In other words, the Japanese firm recruits, allocates, develops, and utilizes its own human resources, relying very little on the outside labor market. Main practices, that stem from this strategy, are listed in the middle box

Table 3-3: Features of Japanese-style Management

Group-orientation (Emphasis on Group Harmony)	The interests of a group are placed over those of an individual. The individual is indentured, body and soul, and loyal to the group.
Community-orientation (Total Concern for People)	The company concerns itself with the private life of its employees as well as their performance at work.
Collective Decision-making by Consensus	The company is willing to share a large amount of information with all employees to allow them to join in decision-making.
Group Duties and Responsibilities	An individual's jobs are not clearly defined, nor duties spelt out in written form; and the responsibility is highly diffused.
Life-time Employment	The employees are guaranteed a job until retirement. The company does not dismiss employees, even when they become redundant.
Comprehensive Welfare Programs	The company provides to all employees total welfare programs, incorporating recreational/medical facilities, housing, company loan, and so on.
Seniority based Pay/Promotion	The length of an employee's service at the company, rather than his ability or performance, is an important criterion in determining pay and promotion.
On-the-job Training	The company provides training programs, that continue late into career, to all employees for the development of skills useful to the company.
Job-rotation	The company rotates the employees to perform different jobs within the company in order to develop the generalist rather than the specialist.

of Figure 3-8. All these practices are inter-related and employed to realize the desired organizational behavior and performance. The outcomes, cited in the last two boxes, are common HRM goals for any company in any country, but the practices actually employed to achieve them are not always the same. In Japan, the first two practices in the middle box are mainly employed to achieve better team-work and organizational commitment, the next three aim to strengthen work motivation, and the last two are related to skill development.

Figure 3-8: A Model of Japanese-style Human Resource Management

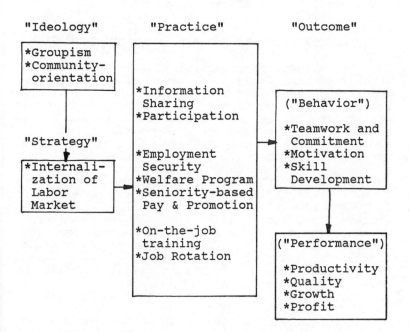

"Ideology"

*Groupism
*Community-orientation

"Strategy"

*Internali-zation of Labor Market

"Practice"

*Information Sharing
*Participation

*Employment Security
*Welfare Program
*Seniority-based Pay & Promotion

*On-the-job training
*Job Rotation

"Outcome"

("Behavior")

*Teamwork and Commitment
*Motivation
*Skill Development

("Performance")

*Productivity
*Quality
*Growth
*Profit

In order to achieve the first set of behavioral outcomes, the management shares information with all employees to allow and encourage them to participate in decision-making. The management also assigns work on a group-to-group basis with vague specification of an individual's duties and responsibilities within the group. To enhance work motivation,

73

the management shows genuine concern for each employee, as reflected in their treatment of the employee as a total person, by offering job security until retirement, providing comprehensive welfare programs, and taking into consideration not only ability but also the length of service in determining his pay and promotion. To develop skills useful to the company and make its employees flexible enough to perform various types of job, the management recruits new employees annually fresh from schools, provides them continuous on-the-job training, and rotates them frequently within the company To sum up, it would seem that the features of Japanese-style management, which are shown in Table 3-3, are all employed in the actual practice of HRM in Japan.

BORROWED CONCEPTS AND INDIGENOUS PRACTICES

In the absence of clearly-formulated theories of management in Japan, we have resorted to the models of Japanese management built upon the facts - the practices of the Japanese-style management of ideas, things, and people. We should recognize that there is no such thing as a typical Japanese company or uniformly accepted management practices. There are wide variations; no one organization contains each and every characteristic that we have identified, in pure form. Nevertheless, virtually all managers of large companies in Japan at least seek to achieve, as nearly as possible, these underlying characteristics. A model is an abstraction from reality; it is a bare-bone attempt to lay out the important and distinctive features of ideas, things, or people. In this sense, the models we have examined here should be useful in gaining our understanding of the indigenousness of Japanese management practices.

Our brief review of the evolution of management theories in the West and the prevailing practices of management in Japan has provided a clear indication that the Japanese have been very successful in putting the imported concepts, albeit modified in varying degrees, into practice. So successful indeed that the very people who had taught these concepts to the Japanese are now attempting to learn something from their students.

Table 3-4: Transplanted Western Concepts of
Management

"Scientific Management"	* Harmonious group action * Cooperation of human beings * Development of all workers for their own and company's prosperity
"Classical Theory"	* Spirit of cooperation * Equity and fair remuneration * Initiative at all levels of organizational ladder * Stability of the tenure of personnel
"Behavioral Sciences"	* Work motivation by social and psychological factors * Democratic leadership patterns * Social skills of managers * Concern for people
"Contingency Theory"	* Organic type of management * Contingency or situational approach to management

To be sure, the Japanese have been extremely selective and have not adopted all the concepts of Western management (e.g. Bureaucracy Theory and, to a lesser extent, Management Sciences). However, they have adopted a great many. Table 3-4 shows a small sample of the Western concepts that the Japanese have actually put into practice.

Needless to say, there is no one best way to explain why these and other foreign concepts have taken root in Japanese organizations. One possible explanation could well be that many of these concepts originally developed in the West have proven to match better with the cultural values of Japanese people than those of people in their land of origin. In the next two chapters, therefore, we shall examine the influence of culture on management in order to gain insights into the transferability of management across cultures.

NOTES

1. Lilienthal, D.E., A Humanist Art, New York: Columbia University Press, (1967), p.18

2. Goode, W.J. and P.K. Hatt, Methods in Social Research, New York: McGraw-Hill, (1952)

3. Drucker, P.F., The Practice of Management, New York: Harper & Row (1954)

4. Mintzberg, H., The Nature of Managerial Work, Englewood Cliffs: Prentice-Hall, (1980)

5. Naroll, P., "Comments to the Authors - Dominant Epistemological Presupposition in the Use of Cross-Cultural Survey Method", Current Anthropology, (Mar. 1975), pp.29-52

6. Koontz, H., "The Management Theory Jungle", Journal of Academy of Management, (Dec. 1961), pp.174-188

7. Koontz, H., C. O'Donnell and H. Weihrich, Management, New York: McGraw-Hill, (1984), pp.31-32

8. Fayol, H., General and Industrial Management, C. Storrs (trans.), London: Sir Issac Pitman & Sons, (1949), p.15

9. Hall, R.H., "Concept of Bureaucracy; An Empirical Assessment", American Journal of Sociology, (Jul. 1963), p.33

10. Barnard, C., The Functions of the Executive, Cambridge, MA: Harvard University Press, (1938), p.73

11. Burns, T. and G.M. Stalker, The Management of Innovation, London: Tavistock Publications, (1961)

12. Lorsch, J.W. and P.R. Lawrence, Studies in Organization Design, Homewood, Ill.: Richard D. Irwin (1970)

13. Kast, F.E. and J.E. Rosenzweig, Organization and Management: A Systems and Contingency Approach, New York: McGraw-Hill, (1982)

14. Koontz, H. et al (1984), op.cit.

15. Yang, C.Y., "Management Styles: American vis-a-vis Japanese", Columbia Journal of World Business, (Fall 1977), pp.23-31

16. MacKenzie, R.A., "The Management Process in 3-D", Harvard Business Review, (Nov./Dec.1969)

17. Koontz, H. and C. O'Donnell, Management: A Systems and Contingency Analysis of Management Functions, New York: McGraw-Hill, (1976)

18. Kono, T., "Summary Results of Mail Survey of Long-Range Planning Practices of Companies in Japan", monograph, Tokyo: Gakushuin University, (Aug. 1979)

19. Hayashi, K., "Corporate Planning Practices in Japanese Multinationals", Academy of Management Journal, (Jun. 1978), pp.211-226

20. Yoshikawa, E., "Organizational Development in Japanese Management" in Uno, M. (ed.), Japanese Managerial Environment ('Nihon-no Keiei Kankyo' in Japanese), Tokyo: Nihon Keizai Shinbun, (1973), pp.141-185

21. Drucker, P.F., (1955), op.cit.

22. Huang, J.C. and R.T. Hsieh, "MBO - A New Concept of Participation: Studies on Workers' Preference in the Republic of China (Taiwan)", Proceedings of the Conference of the Academy of International Business - South East Asia region, (1986), pp.101-113

23. Mintzberg, H., "The Manager's Job: Folklore and Fact", Harvard Business Review, (Jul./Aug.1975), p.50

24. Simon H.A., The New Science of Management Decision, New York: Harper & Row, (1960)

25. Hattorri, I., "A Proposition on Efficient Decision-Making in Japanese Corporation", Columbia Journal of World Business, (Summer 1978), pp.7-15

26. Fox, W.M., "Japanese Management: Tradition under Strain", Business Horizon, (Aug. 1977), pp.76-85

27. Iwata, R., Japanese-style Management, Tokyo: Asian Productivity Organization, (1982)

28. ibid.

29. Campbell, D.J., "The Meaning of Work: American and Japanese Paradigms", Asian Pacific Journal of Management, (Sept. 1985), pp.1-9

30. Morita, A., Made in Japan London: Collins, (1987)

31. Ishida, H., "Transferability of Japanese Human Resource Management Abroad", Human Resource Management (Spring 1986), pp.103-120

32. ibid.

Chapter Four

THE INFLUENCE OF CULTURE ON MANAGEMENT: HOW SIGNIFICANT IS IT?

Important cultural underpinnings of Japanese management are said to be groupism and a vertical structural tendency, which are found in Japanese society at large. The Japanese believe their society as culturally unique. Undermining the logic of industrialization that should have resulted in similarities among the industrialized nations regardless of their cultural traditions, Japan's cultural uniqueness is manifested in a variety of organizational and behavioral phenomena today. In fact, many of the features of Japanese management as described in the previous chapter could be explained in terms of Japan's deeply-rooted cultural values, which are quite distinct from those held in the West or even its neighboring countries in East Asia. In this chapter, we will first look at the East and West contrast in cultural orientations. That will be followed by detailed examination of the implications of cultural values for Japanese management practices. Chapter Five will then look beyond Japan's national boundary, and analyze the similarities as well as differences among East Asian countries which have a common heritage yet divergent cultural values.

EAST AND WEST CONTRAST

The characteristics of Oriental management practices which contrast with those of the West have been noted by many researchers. For example, Redding and Martyn-Johns advanced and partly tested a set of hypotheses through a survey of managerial beliefs in Southeast Asian countries [1]. The hypotheses included:

a) Managerial decisions in Oriental companies will take greater account of effects on the relative status of other people than in Western companies.
b) Oriental companies will use either less formal planning systems and/or planning systems with fewer variables than the equivalent Western companies.
c) In Oriental companies, the degree of formal organization will be less than in equivalent Western companies.
d) The style of leadership employed by Oriental managers will rely less on interpersonal confrontations with subordinates than would be the case with Western managers.
e) The control of performance in Oriental companies will be less formal than the Western equivalents.

These differences in management practices between East and West might be explained by cultural orientations. Adler gives six basic dimensions that describe the cultural orientations of societies, each of which reflect a value with attitudinal and behavioral implications [2]. As shown in Table 4-1, these dimensions are:

* People's nature as individuals ("Who am I?")
* Their relationship to nature and the world ("How do I see the world?")
* Their relationship to other people ("How do I relate to other people?")
* Their primary type of activity ("What do I do?")
* Their orientation in time and space ("How do I use time and space?")

People's orientations in the given dimensions differ, to a considerable degree, across cultures. The Japanese, for example, are rather close to those shown in the first column, whereas the American orientations tend to be close to those shown in the second column. Societies which consider people "good" are inclined to trust people a great deal; societies which consider people "evil" suspect and mistrust them. Americans generally see people as a mixture of good and evil, capable of choosing one over the other. Americans also see themselves as dominant over nature and want to control nature,

79

Table 4-1: Cultural Dimensions and Orientations

Cultural Dimension	Cultural Orientation		
Nature of People	Good	Good & Evil	Evil
Relationship to Nature	Harmony	Dominant	Subjugation
Relationship to Other People	Hierarchical Groups	Individuals	Laterally Extended Groups
Primary Type of Activity	Controlling	Doing	Being
Time Orientation	Future	Present	Past
Space Orientation	Public	Private	Mixed

[Adapted from Adler, N.J., 1986, p.12]

whereas the Japanese want to live in harmony with nature. In some other countries, notably in the Islamic societies, people see themselves subjugated by nature and accept the inevitable forces of nature.

In individual-oriented societies such as the US, people value the individual's welfare over that of the group. By contrast, in group-oriented societies such as Japan, people value the group's welfare over that of the individual, placing relatively great emphasis on group harmony, unity, and loyalty. The US is a doing-oriented society, where people stress accomplishments measured by objective standards; however, in control-oriented societies such as Japan, people restrain their own desires to allow each individual to develop an integrated whole. On the other hand, people in being-oriented societies stress release and indulgence of existing desires.

Future-oriented cultures believe that plans should be evaluated in terms of the projected future benefits to be gained from a specific action. By contrast, past-oriented cultures believe that plans should be evaluated in terms of the customs and traditions of society. Most European countries are past-oriented; Japan has a relatively long-term, future-oriented time horizon; and the US generally focuses on the present and near future. People's conceptions of space are also different across cultures. Americans emphasize the private use of physical space, whereas the Japanese are rather public-oriented both at home and work.

American business is the product of Western culture, which rests upon Judeo-Christian theism. Western culture conceives society from a spiritual point of view. It places great emphasis on the divinity of man's identity, rights, and obligations. It holds work to be a divine demand upon one's talents; it also holds business success, although gained through hard work, to be evidence of divine favor and selection. American society and business adhere to these spiritual values. On the other hand, Japanese business is the product of a different culture, to a large extent based on the teachings of Confucius - a non-theistic philosophy that puts high priority upon love, propriety, faithfulness, and righteousness in human relations as well as wisdom to be gained from education. Japanese culture thus conceives society from a humanistic rather than spiritural point of view. It fixes man's role in the society in relation to other people, placing high value on reciprocity, harmony, and loyalty to the society and to one's work group. Japanese society and business have grown and flourished through adherence to these humanistic values.

CULTURAL CLUSTERS

A survey of 2,800 managers from eleven countries, conducted in the early 1960s by three American psychologists, indicated that there were not large, insuperable differences in beliefs about leadership among the countries [3]. All eleven countries clustered low on the beliefs in the individual's innate capacity for initiative and leadership, and high but roughly together on the beliefs in sharing information and objectives, participative management, and internal control rather than external control. The survey also revealed a remarkable agreement among countries in their perception of the role a manager played. To cooperate was thought to be most important, to direct was a close second, to persuade was next, and finally, to reprimand was the least important. The same order held roughly for goodness; cooperation and direction were perceived very good, persuasion somewhat less so, and reprimanding the least of all. Difficulty, however, was another story; directing was the hardest thing to do, persuading was next hardest, reprimanding was easier but cooperating was slightly easier still.

It is of particular significance that the survey indicated that the beliefs about leadership and patterns in the managerial role were more or less explicable in terms of cultural traditions rather than the degree or kind of industrialization in the countries. In fact, within a rather homogeneous set of responses, the consistent groupings of countries were found - the Anglo-Saxon pair, Continental (Latin) Europe, Northern (Teutonic) Europe, and Japan. Several other studies of managerial and workforce values have identified at least six distinguishable clusters of countries, each showing strong similarities in the values that seemed to be based on a common cultural heritage. The six clusters are:

a) Anglo-American,
b) Northern European,
c) Central European,
d) Southern European,
e) Latin American, and
f) East Asian.

Hofstede conducted one of the most influential studies of this kind in a US-based multinational company operating in more than forty countries [4]. The four cultural dimensions used in his study are explained in Table 4-2.

Table 4-2: Four Cultural Dimensions

Power Distance	The degree to which a society accepts a hierarchical or unequal distribution of power in organizations.
Uncertainty Avoidance	The degree to which a society perceives ambiguous and uncertain situations as threatening and as things to be avoided.
Individualism	The degree to which a society prefers a loosely knit social framework in which individuals take care of themselves and their immediate family only. The opposite, "collectivism", refers to situations where individuals expect their relatives, clans, or other in-groups to look after them, in exchange for unquestioning loyalty.
Masculinity	The degree to which a society emphasizes often stereotyped masculine traits such as assertiveness, independence, and insensitivity to feelings as dominant values. The opposite, "femininity", refers to the extent to which preferences for relationships, modesty, caring for the weak, and the quality of life are prevalent in social and organizational life.

Of the four dimensions, power distance and individualism are particularly useful in discovering sharp contrast between East and West (see Figure 4-1). Power distance refers to dependence on more powerful people; and individualism refers to independence from groups, organizations, or collectivism. Although the two dimensions are conceptually different, there seems to exist a broad overall correlation between them. East Asian societies (e.g. Japan, South Korea, Taiwan, Hong Kong, and Singapore) fall into the quadrant which is characterized by high power distance and collectivism, whereas all Anglo-American societies (e.g. the US, the UK, Australia, and Canada) fall into the diagonally opposite quadrant.

Figure 4-1: Power-Distance and Individualism Scale

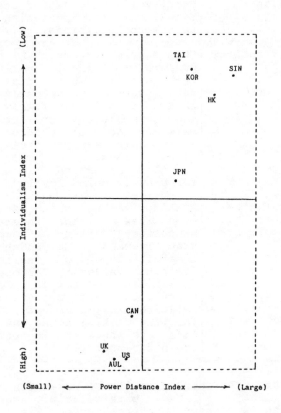

[Adapted from Hofstede, G., 1984, p.159, and from Hofstede, G., "Cultural Differences in Teaching and Learning", paper presented at the Colloquium on Selected Issues in International Business, Honolulu, Hawaii, Aug. 1985]

In essence, findings from cultural cluster research have suggested the neat division in value terms between East and West. Considering a sizable influence of cultural values on the behavior of people in a given country, it could be well argued that the management principles, previously held to be universally applicable, are not suitable to all cultural clusters. For example, the Motivation Theories, developed largely in the Anglo-American context, may need to be substantially revised for East Asia. Self-actualization needs, as explained by Maslow [5], seem more a reflection of an individualistic culture than a collectivist culture. Similarly, the Western Theories of Leadership may need to be modified considerably for East Asia, where people tend to value high power distance rather than egalitarianism [6]. The issues regarding the applicability of these Western theories to East Asia will be discussed in some detail in Chapter Seven.

CULTURAL UNDERPINNING OF JAPANESE MANAGEMENT

There is a hypothetical logic of industrialization which leads to similarities among the industrialized nations regardless of the cultural traditions of the pre-industrialized society [7]. Included as a universal feature of the logic is worldwide industrialization, which occurs through the transfer of technology, particularly knowledge technology, including the management knowledge and knowhow. Such transfer, in pursuit of industrialization, has surely helped create many similarities in management practices among the industrialized nations. Pascale's study, for example, revealed substantial similarities in two culturally very different but equally industrialized nations - Japan and the US [8]. However, in his reappraisal of the logic of Convergence Theory, Jamieson remarked [9]:

> It would be foolish to deny that there are great similarities to be found in the social structures of many industrialized societies, but this is not to admit that the reasons for this are imperatives of industrialization.
>   [Jamieson, I., 1980, p.4]

85

He pointed out that the formal rationality allegedly built into the industrialization process did not spread to other institutions of society. In other words, the transfer of technology did not necessarily lead to a total assimilation among all industrialized nations. Whitehill and Takezawa have noted that the Japanese have not tried to assimilate all American ideas and methods; they have remained highly selective, even cautious, particularly in those areas where they see little need for imported change [10].

The overwhelming majority of Japanese view their society as culturally unique. The cultural uniqueness, manifested in a variety of organizational and behavioral phenomena, persists as an enduring characteristic of Japanese society, despite the logic of world-wide industrialization. The Japanese company may have a formal organization chart, that shows a hierarchical structure very similar to a typical American company. But the behavior of Japanese managers does not reflect the hierarchy as closely as in most American companies. While some of the similarities in management practices around the world may be explained in terms of industrialization, the differences may need to be explained in terms of cultural variables. The influence of culture on management practices, especially on those related to managing the social system in an organization, is considerable.

One of the most important cultural underpinnings of Japanese management is groupism - a strong sense of attachment to the group. Many Japanese identify their native characteristics as stemming from the Tokugawa era (1603 - 1867 A.D.) - the period immediately preceding the modernization of Japan. During that era and thereafter, the Japanese had come to believe that [11]:

* An individual receives a continuous flow of blessings that establish obligations within groups,
* Social, political, ethical, and religious norms are of value only as they are valuable to groups,
* Values are achieved in groups, and

* All the values are endowed with an almost
  sacred Japanese quality and are best
  implemented by, or in the name of, symbolic
  head of family-style groups.

To date, attachment to the group has remained a
value commonly shared by the Japanese. Vogel
refers to this phenomenon as a "Continuing Value
Consensus" [12].

Such a strong sense of attachment to the
group may be explained, at least in part, by the
Japanese holistic view of sociey, that is also
generally held in other East Asian cultures. The
holistic view reflects the influence of several
schools of Eastern philosophy including Taoism
and, especially, Zen Buddhism [13]. Beginning
with the notion that ultimate reality is an
all-embracing unity from which nothing can be
separated, the Taoist sages have suggested that
this ultimate reality must reside within the self
and can be discovered through meditation [14].
Zen Buddhism also embodies the idea that
introspection, through meditation, can lead to
enlightenment. The physicist Capra has observed
that the most important characteristic of the
Oriental view is the awareness of the unity and
mutual interaction of all things and events,
which are interdependent and inseparable parts of
the whole. In comparing the Eastern and Western
views, he has noted that contrary to the Western
view which tends to divide the perceived world
into individual and separate things, the division
of nature into separate objects is not fundamental in the Eastern view and any such objects
have a fluid and everchanging character [15].

In contrast to the Western logical process
of seeking to classify, categorize, and
conceptualize everything, harmony is a fundamental principle in the Oriental culture.
Murayama distinguishes what is termed
"undirectional causal paradigm" typical of
Western thinking and "mutual causal paradigm"
which typifies Eastern thinking [16]. The former
is related to classificational, quantitative,
anthropocentric, and competitive social organization and perception; the latter is contextual,
polyocular, process-oriented, and harmonistic
social organization and perception. Northrop
supports this process difference by suggesting
that the West developed logical realism, which is
knowledge of tested abstract relationships

between the observed things, matters or events;
it has a relational and sequential logic. By
contrast, the East developed radical empiricism
with an equally consistent body of knowledge, but
with a different foundation and direction; an
abstract framework does not exist, and knowledge
is derived by the intermingling of the observers'
perception and the total situation [17].

Some writers have suggested that cognitive
styles are different in Eastern and Western
cultures. Cognitive style refers to the process
through which an individual resolves differences
between an internalized view of the environment
and what is actually perceived in the same
environment. There is clinical and experimental
evidence about the hemispheric specialization of
the human brain; the left side of the brain
favors rational, analytical processing, while the
right side utilizes intuitive, spatial processing
[18]. The analytical left hemisphere carries on
the humdrum, practical, everyday work of the
brain, while the intuitive right hemisphere
is mainly responsible for those flights of
imagination that produce great art, great
science, and great management.

However, evidence provided by the research
does not in any way imply that either hemisphere
is capable of problem solving independent of the
other. There is still some evidence for the very
plausible hypothesis that some people, confronted
with a particular problem, make more use of the
intuitive process in solving it, while other
people make relatively more use of the analytical
process [19]. Although individuals should be
equally adept at both kinds of processing,
factors such as culture, experience, and
education lead us to prefer one to the other.
Mintzberg, who had undertaken a study on
relationships between culture and cognitive
style, found that the right hemispheric
processing was more dominant in Eastern culture
[20]. Several other cross-cultural management
studies on the cognitive styles of American,
Japanese, Chinese, and Korean managers have
confirmed his finding [21].

Another equally important cultural
underpinning of Japanese management is a vertical
structural tendency. Nakane, the Japanese social
anthropologist, describes Japanese society as
organic and vertically related [22]. This view

of the society has also stemmed from the Tokugawa era. The rulers of the era found a useful ideology in Confucianism which concerns itself mainly with the correct observance of social relationships in a hierarchically-structured society. We consequently find in Tokugawa Japan a very rigid and vertically structured society with a strong emphasis on authoritarian control on the one hand and obedience on the other, giving rise to a series of highly regulated patterns of inter-personal relationships. Central to the concept of vertical relationship is the idea that belonging to an organization is far more important than affiliation across a horizontally-structured professional field. Therefore, a member of the organization tends to identify himself with the company he works for than with his profession.

IMPLICATIONS OF CULTURAL VALUES

The two main characteristics of Japanese society (i.e. groupism and vertical relation) can be attributed to the deeply-rooted cultural values. Values are sets of interrelated ideas, concepts, and principles to which individuals, groups, and societies attach strong sentiments; they generate expected rules of behavior when they are applied to a specific culture. As shown in Table 4-3, the core values of Japanese culture, most commonly cited by the management writers, are "ninjo" (human feeling), "amae" (dependence), "on" (favor/debt), and "giri" (mutual duty) [23]. The recognition of these interrelated values as the desirable explains why the Japanese have a strong sense of attachment to groups and are willing to accept a mutually-binding vertical relationship within the group. In Chapter Three, we have examined several models of Japanese management. Based on a premise that the cultural values commonly held in a society have an important bearing on management practices, let us now see if we can identify any patterns of relationships between these cultural values and the management as practiced in Japan.

Table 4-3: Core Values of Japanese Culture

"Ninjo" (Human Feeling)	A feeling which spontaneously occurs and includes all human impulses and inclinations.
"Amae" (Dependence)	A feeling of dependence, which is a state of mind that describes a desire to be passively loved (or spoiled), a desire to be protected from the world of objective reality.
"On" (Favor/Debt)	A favor handed down or debt of gratitude as a result of receiving a favor. One receives an "on" (favor); one carries an "on" (debt). "On" are obligations from the point of view of the passive recipient; the obligation incurred by "on" can never be completely repaid.
"Giri" (Mutual Duty)	A mutual and reciprocal obligation that must be repaid. "Giri" is a relationship of interdependence brought out by "on", a bond of moral duty.

"Ninjo" and "amae"-based interpersonal relationships assume a high degree of emotional attachment that will often lead the group to make a seemingly irrational decision and avoid pinpointing the consequence of a decision to any particular individual for the sake of group harmony. Furthermore, "on" and "giri" within the group are exacting and rigorously binding. The relationship once established becomes sacred and maintained, though it may be seen as purely emotional in the Western sense. In explaining the features of Japanese management attributable to these core values of Japanese culture, Morita stated [24]:

The most important mission for a
Japanese manager is to develop a healthy
relationship with his employees, to
create a family-like feeling within the
corporation, a feeling that employees
and managers share the same fate ...
Sometimes it is more important to
generate a sense of affinity than
anything else, and sometimes you must
make decisions that are, technically,
irrational. You can be totally rational
with a machine. But if you work with
people, sometimes logic has to take a
backseat to understanding.

[Morita, A., 1987, p.130]

Along the rational/irrational spectrum, the
majority of Western theorists have long held a
view that managerial decision-making should be a
conscious, rational process in which the manager
selects a set of criteria and uses it to evaluate
alternative solutions to a particular problem.
However, as the Japanese see it, decision-making
could be an irrational and emotional process.
Simon has described the process managers use to
make decisions as bounded rationality [25].
According to Simon, managers make choices based
on simplified rather than real situations. The
subjective rationality thus narrows and alters
the objective facts. Managers from different
cultures perceive the world differently, and
their subjective rationalities are different, as
are their ways of simplifying complex realities
in environments in which they are to make
choices.

In other words, decision-making is
culturally contingent; that is, the best way to
make a decision depends on the values, attitudes,
and behavioral patterns of the people involved.
In a holistic culture such as Japan, people
discuss all alternatives before making a
decision, while in other sequence-oriented
cultures such as the US people tend to discuss
alternatives in a preplanned sequence, making
incremental decisions as they go along. American
managers generally process facts and make
decisions by questioning whether an alternative
is correct or incorrect; Japanese mangers
question whether an alternative is good or bad.
The former orient themselves around a belief in

absolute truth, whereas the latter orient themselves around a fit between the choice and what they are trying to accomplish.

The essence of the core values of Japanese culture, that significantly affect managerial decision-making, can be explained in terms of the traditional and ubiquitous concept of "ie" (household). The "ie" is a social group constructed on the basis of an established frame of residence and also of business organization. The core of this concept is found in the vertical relationships among the members of the traditional Japanese household. On the surface, the formal authority appears to be heavily concentrated in the head of the household but, being anxious to maintain "wa" (harmony), the head of the household more often than not consults with the key members of his household when making important decisions.

This emphasis on group harmony, observed in a traditional household of related members, is also evident in an artificial or simulated kinship group of unrelated individuals such as a business organization. As clearly reflected in the "ringi" system of decision-making, important decisions are made not by any particular individual possessing a formal authority but collectively by a group of people. And the task is assigned to a group, with vague specification of an individual's duties and responsibilities within the group. Responsibility for decisions is, therefore, highly diffused; even the chief executive can absolve himself of responsibility on the ground that he has acted on the basis of prior consensus reached among his subordinates. Under this system, consensus is all important and group-consciouness is stressed. The rigor and formality of the system suggests an underlying discipline, and respect for status is preserved in the ritualistic rise of an idea through the vertically-structured organization.

The adoption of such a system of decision-making in Japan is essential, because conflicts among the members of a group are more disruptive to the smooth attainment of goals in a collectivity-oriented society than in an individualistic society. In comparing Japanese and American organizational characteristics, Ouchi and Jaeger pointed out [26]:

> The organizational ideal for the US has
> developed in a culture which supports
> norms of independence, self-reliance,
> and individual responsibility. By
> contrast, the deal for Japan has evolved
> in a culture which supports norms of
> collectivism.
> [Ouchi, W.G. and A.M. Jaeger, 1978, p.309]

The American decision-making process is individualistic, whereas the Japanese process relies on the consensus of all members involved. The creation of informal, affective interpersonal relations between the leader and his subordinates is very much encouraged in Japan. The leader not only admits dependence on subordinates but actually uses this situation to strengthen relations with them. In other words, the role of the manager in Japan is one of the facilitator rather than the decision-maker, in the Western sense; and his main job is to foster group strengths by maintaining harmony in his organization. It is generally believed that the qualities of an effective leader in Japan's group-oriented and vertically-structured society are as follows [27]:

a) Activate the group's energy to the fullest by appearing to be unaware of what is going on, while actually being in complete command of the situation.
b) Reward subordinates, who follow the rules of "giri" and "ninjo", with upward climb to success.
c) Place his trusted followers about him skilfully, forming a protective wall around himself.
d) Have the skill to instruct subordinates without putting the instructions into words.

These qualifications can be further summed up into the delegation of authority. In other words, an efective Japanese leader, rather than expressing his own wishes explicitly, delegates his authority, thereby giving his subordinates a sense of importance and satisfaction.

The core values of Japanese culture have no doubt provided far-reaching implications for the practices of management in contemporary Japan. For one thing, a relative lack of well-formulated

long-range plans can be explained, in large part,
by a fear that systematic planning, guided by a
concept like Management by Objectives, will lead
to the weakening or even the destruction of the
collectivity itself. Even when there are long-
range plans of a strategic nature, they are
not always used as a basis for performance
evaluation. A lack of an explicit and formal
control mechanism could be further explained by
the perceived difficulty to include in a plan
such factors as the contribution to group harmony
and cultivation of certain morale-creating interpersonal relationships.

RELATIONSHIPS BETWEEN CULTURE AND MANAGEMENT

The characteristics of Japanese-style human
resource management could also be traced to the
deeply-rooted cultural values. The Japanese are
not governed by logic but rather by the spirit of
"on"(favor/debt), which usually interrelate
"giri"(mutual duty) and "ninjo" (human feeling).
In other words, the sense of social obligation
and human feeling govern Japan's group-oriented
society. Many Japanese believe that "giri" and
"ninjo" are the most important factors in human
relations, and regard them as an unwritten law
which ensures the harmonious functioning of
individuals in a group. "Giri-ninjo" is a sort
of natural contract that the Japanese live by;
the rules and regulations are not formally
committed to writing.

Masatsugu describes Japan as the "On-tract"
society in contrast to the "contract" society of
the West [28]. There are over 500,000 lawyers in
the US compared to approximately 17,000 in
Japan. This means, taking the relative size of
the two countries into account (240 million vs.
120 million), the US has nearly sixty times more
lawyers than Japan. Noting the instrusion of
lawyers and the legal mentality into many facets
of American business, Morita stated that the
lawyer had become a major symbol of the
difference between Japanese and American
management philosophies and style [29].

While the concept of groupism is expressed
in the group-oriented ideology, the concept of
the vertical relationship is expressed in the
community-oriented ideology that also charac-

terizes Japanese style management. "Amae" (a feeling of dependence) governs Japan's vertically-structured society. The verb "amaeru" is derived from the adjective "amai", which literally means "sweet", but is figuratively used to describe self-indulgent behavior in a situation where there is some special relationship between two people or groups. The basic attitude of Japanese employers is parental; the relationship between them and their employees resembles that of a fraternal order. The employer looks upon his employees as a father does his children. The company's concern over the life of all employees extends far beyond the workplace itself. A strong sense of attachment to the group held by employees is thus fostered by efforts made by the company to safeguard its employees' well-being both within and outside the company. In other words, the total loyalty of Japanese employees to their company is reciprocated by the company's total concern for its people. The group and community-oriented ideologies provide strong support for the practices such as the life-time employment system, welfare programs, seniority-based pay and promotion system, on-the-job training, and job-rotation

Life-time employment and seniority-based pay/promotion systems are generally considered as two main pillars of business organizations in Japan. The life-time employment system was introduced in the early 1900s to improve the consciousness of blue-collar workers and reduce the rate of turnover in the factories, that was then quite high. Since its introduction, the system, that offers workers total job security, has taken firm root in Japanese industrial society largely because it matched the cultural traditions of Japanese society. The life-time employment system has made the work group the most cohesive one in an individual person's life. This would not have been possible without a strong partner to sustain it; this partner has been the seniority-based pay and promotion system. As a matter of fact, these two systems are much like the two wheels of a cart; one cannot run without the other - the seniority system supports the life-time employment system, because it rewards employees based on the length of service in the company; the life-time employment system supports the seniority system, because it regulates the hierarchical order and helps maintain group harmony among employees.

In turn, these two systems together provide necessary support for a long-range plan for training employees in specific skills and for broadening their proficiency to become generalists. On-the-job training through job rotation is also used to counterbalance the life-time employment and seniority systems, under which employees would almost certainly become bored by their jobs or demoralized by slow promotions after so many years of work at the same company. Furthermore, as a part of the comprehensive welfare program, many companies offer a wide range of training courses, not necessarily related to job content, for employees and their families (e.g. flower arrangement, tea ceremony, cooking, singing, dancing). These courses are aimed to develop cultured, well-mannered employees who can live and work harmoniously with others in groups.

Unquestionably, the ideologies founded upon Japan's deeply-rooted cultural values provide strong support for the practices of Japanese-style management. However, it would be naive to assume that the unique features of Japanese management are only attributable to the culture [30]. For example, Japanese companies generally spend much more resources to run on-the-job training through job-rotation than their counterparts in the West. However, unless there is some degree of assurance that the employees trained at the company expense will stay long enough to recoup the cost, it is not economically feasible for the company to foot the bill for such a program. The life-time employment system and comprehensive welfare programs, which are to provide continued employment and to improve the livelihood of employees, may therefore be viewed not necessarily as something attributable to the culture but rather as a result of conscious efforts on the part of employers to keep their labor turnover to a minimum. In the same vein, it is possible to interpret the seniority-based remuneration and promotion system as a means of controlling the labor turnover. It could also be argued that employees' economic incentives such as job and income security, rather than their cultural values, would make them stay with the same company for a life-time. Such incentives are commensurate to a strong demand for a high degree of loyalty placed on employees by their employer.

It could be argued that certain features of Japanese-style management are largely attributable to Japan's cultural values, while some others are relatively more attributable to economic incentives. Kono maintains that the former are hard to transfer abroad, whereas the latter are relatively easy [31]. As shown in Table 4-4, those hard-to-transfer features include the ideologies of Japanese enterprises and two closely associated practices of management (i.e. collective decision-making by consensus; group, rather than individual, duties and responsibilities).

Table 4-4: Cultural Values versus Economic Incentives

Features Largely Attributable to Cultural Values	Features Relatively More Attributable to Economic Incentives
Group-orientation	Life-time Employment
Community-orientation	Comprehensive Welfare Programs
Collective Decision-making by Consensus	Seniority-based Pay and Promotion
Group, rather than individual, Duties and Responsibilities	On-the-job Training
	Job Rotation

To sum up, the values of Japan's national culture affect the values of organizational culture, as typically expressed in the ideologies of Japanese enterprises. The ideologies, in turn, affect the practices of management in varying degrees; corporate ideologies also affect and, at times, enhance the values of national culture. The practices thus employed would then need to be reinforced by beliefs and attitudes commonly held in the country (i.e. the values of national culture) in order for the enterprise to achieve its desired outcomes. Admittedly, it is difficult to determine the exact causal linkage between culture and management. Nevertheless, there seem to exist certain patterns of relationship between the two.

Notes

1. Reading, S.G. and T.A. Martyn-Johns, "Paradigm Differences and Their Relations to Management, with References to Southeast Asia" in England, G.W., A.R. Negandhi and B. Wilpert (eds.), Organizational Functioning in a Cross-Cultural Perspective, Kent: Comparative Administration Research Institute, (1979), pp.103-125

2. Adler, N.J., International Dimensions of Organizational Behavior, Boston: Kent Publishing Co., (1986)

3. Haire, M., E.E. Ghiselli and L.W. Porter, Managerial Thinking: An International Study, New York: John Wiley & Sons, (1966)

4. Hofstede, G., Culture's Consequences: International Differences in Work-related Values, Beverly Hills, CA: Sage Publications, (1984)

5. Maslow, A.H., "A Theory of Human Motivation", Psychological Review, (Jul. 1943), pp.370-396

6. Dunphy, D.C., "The Comparative Study of Managerial Behavior in East Asia and the West", Proceedings of the Academy of International Business (Southeast Asia region) Conference, (Jun. 1986), pp.645-663

7. Dunning, E.G. and E.I. Hopper, "Industrialization and the Problem of Convergence: A Critical Note", The Sociological Review, (Jul. 1966), pp.163-186

8. Pascale, R.T., "Communication and Decision Making Across Cultures: Japanese and American Comparisons", Administrative Science Quarterly, (Mar. 1978), pp.91-110

9. Jamieson, I., Capitalism and Culture, London: Gower, (1980)

10. Whitehill, A.M. and S. Takezawa, "Workingplace Harmony: Another Japanese Miracle?", Columbia Journal of World Business, (Fall 1978), pp.25-39

11. Burks, A.W. <u>Japan: Profile of a Post-industrial Power</u>, Boulder, Colorado: Westview Press, (1981)

12. Vogel, E., <u>Japan's New Middle Class</u>, Berkeley, CA: University of California Press, (1965)

13. Namamura, H., "Japan: Religion and Philosophy" in Cornish, G. (ed.), <u>Encyclopedia Americana</u>, (1970), vol. 15, pp.713-719

14. Blakney, R., <u>The Way of Life: Lao Tzu</u>, New York: Mentor Books, (1964)

15. Capra, F., <u>The Tao of Physics</u>, London: Wildwood House, (1975)

16. Murayama, M., "Paradigmotslogy and Its Application to Cross-Disciplinary, Cross-Professional, and Cross-Cultural Communication", <u>Dialectics</u>, (1974), vol.28, no.3, pp.135-196

17. Northrop, F.S.C., <u>The Meeting of East and West</u>, New York: Macmillan, (1946)

18. Robey, D. and W. Taggart, "Human Information Processing in Information and Decision Support Systems", <u>MIS Quarterly</u>, (Jun. 1982), pp.61-73

19. Doktor, R.H., "Problem Solving Styles of Executives and Management Scientists" in Charnes, A., W.W. Cooper and R.J. Niehaus (eds.), <u>Management Science Approach to Manpower Planning and Organization Design</u>, Amsterdam: North-Holland, (1978)

20. Mintzberg, H., "Planning on the Left Side and Managing on the Right", <u>Harvard Business Review</u>, (Jul./Aug. 1976), pp.3-9

21. Sherling, S.A., S.C. Ho, J.P. Cragin, M.T. Basuray and B.J. Ederhardt, "Eastern and Western Cognitive Preferences", <u>Proceedings of the Academy of International Business (Southeast Asia region) Conference</u>, (Jul. 1985), pp.119-128

22. Nakane, C., <u>Japanese Society</u>, London: Weidenfeld & Nicolson, (1970)

23. Sethi, S.P., N. Namiki and C.L. Swanson, <u>The False Promise of Japanese Miracle</u>, London: Pitman, (1984); Masatsugu, M., <u>Management and Society - Lessons from Contemporary Japan</u>, Singapore: Federal Publications, (1985)

24. Morita, A., <u>Made in Japan</u>, London: Collins, (1987)

25. Simon, H.A., <u>Administrative Behavior</u>, New York: Free Press, (1957)

26. Ouchi, W.G. and A.M. Jaeger, "Type Z Organization: Stability in the Midst of Mobility", <u>Academy of Management Review</u>, (Apr. 1978), pp.305-314

27. Masatsugu, M., (1985), op.cit.

28. ibid.

29. Morita, A., (1987), op.cit.

30. Umetani, S., "The Japanese Management: Personnel Management Process, Manpower Development and Managerial Efficiency", paper presented at the International Management Development Congress, (Hong Kong, Jan. 1986)

31. Kono, T., "Japanese Management Philosophy: Can It be Exported?", <u>Long Range Planning</u>, (Jun. 1982), pp.90-102

Chapter Five

MANAGEMENT PRACTICES IN EAST ASIAN CULTURAL
SETTINGS: ARE THEY ALL THE SAME?

Japan and Asia's four other industrialized
countries (i.e. South Korea, Taiwan, Hong Kong,
and Singapore), together with ASEAN countries and
the People's Republic of China (PRC), are
geographically categorized as East Asia. East
Asia has one-third of the world's population, and
consists of different political, economic, and
social systems. Yet, in discussing management
practices, quite often the Orientals are simply
lumped together based on an assumption that
people in the region, especially those living in
Asia's five industrialized countries, share a
common value system codified in Confucianism.
Would it be correct to assume that the sharing of
such a value system, coupled with the use of a
common (or at least similar) language, a racial
similarity, a geographical proximity, or any
other things, which appear to link these people,
are powerful enough to make their practices of
management the same? The answer is an emphatical
"no". Even the once-common Confucian system of
thoughts has been interpreted differently and
diverged over centuries. Perhaps nowhere is this
more clear than in the contrast between the
Japanese and the Chinese. In this chapter, we
will first look at the similarities and
differences in cultural values between the
Japanese and the Chinese, and then go on to
examine the patterns of relationships between
culture and management within the East Asian
context.

DIVERSITY IN CULTURAL VALUES

When talking about the Chinese, we must ask
ourselves "What kind of Chinese?" The vast
majority of the Chinese live in the mainland -
the People's Republic of China (PRC). They are

at present experimenting with a new kind of
management system that is based on a combination
of the socialistic and capitalistic ideologies.
The rapid changes and yet unknown outcome of the
on-going experiment would make the study of their
management system extremely difficult (see
Appendix "Chinese Management: Whatever Happened
to Its Tradition?" to get a glimpse of the
management system in the PRC today). Besides
more than one billion Chinese living in the
mainland, there are millions of overseas Chinese
spread throughout the Southeast Asian region.
They live under systems totally different from
that in the PRC. The overseas Chinese norm is
the small-scale family business. This form
dominates not only the economies of their
principal bases (i.e. Taiwan, Hong Kong, and
Singapore) but also those of Thailand, Malaysia,
Indonesia, the Philippines, and so forth. For
the sake of simplicity and practicality, the term
"Chinese" used in this book mostly refers to the
Overseas Chinese.

To be sure, the region, where many overseas
Chinese reside today, is very much diversified in
terms of cultural backgrounds. In Thailand where
51 million people live, one finds a culture of
easy-going and happy people. It is assumed that
the original Thais migrated southward from South
Central China around the 5th to 7th centuries;
and Buddhism was introduced from India in the
13th century. Accordingly, Thai culture origi-
nated from a mixture of Chinese and Indian
influences, although it would be difficult to say
exactly when one began and the other left off.
The two have become intertwined into a single
entity that is distinctly Thai. The basic
philosophy of the Thai people is an attitude that
has led them to accept a very rigid class system,
in which people acknowledge their position
relative to others. The value orientation of
Thai people is more toward cozy, comfortable
human relationships than self-sacrifice for the
group. The orientation of enjoying one's life
does not help foster a strong sense of attachment
to the group. Thais conduct their lives on a
self-centered basis. For one thing, they do not
always seek the attention of their supervisors
but look out for their own self interests [1].
In this sense, then, we could say that Thais are
rather individual-oriented.

On the map, Malaysia (population 16 million) is hanging down below Thailand and snuggling up to the huge Indonesian island of Sumatra to the West. In terms of population, 54 per cent are native Malays; 35 per cent are Chinese, who had migrated in large scale from China's southern coast in the middle of the 19th century; 10 per cent are Indians. Culturally, the Hindu influence had been strong until the arrival of Islam from northern Sumatra in the 15th century. Islam eventually became established as the majority religion and gradually the notions of modern Malay culture began to evolve. In contrast to the Buddhist Thais, who put a high priority on an easy and happy life, the Malay people consider the effort to enjoy one's own life as possessing very low value. Their value system is much influenced by the concept of fatalism and Islam. Fatalism makes it possible to accept almost anything through a sense of resignation and tolerance. Islam teaches moderation and implants a strong sense of prudence. Malays, therefore, tend to take an indifferent attitude, not wanting to intrude on others and not be interfered with by others [2]. Under this type of value system, the Malay society is characterized as self-reserved and not causing unpleasant feelings in others; good manners mean to criticize as little as possible. Formality is considered as having a high priority; and as long as form is arranged, even if the essentials are not met, it is still permissible.

Indonesia is the home of over 360 tribal and ethnic groups. Yet the Indonesians have certain traits in common. Most of them are basically Malay in ethnic background, and 90 per cent of the total population (170 million) are Islams. Like Malays, the Indonesian people also tend to regard their life as predetermined. However, in contrast to the Malays, whose orientation is rather fatalistic, the Indonesians tend to be reality and individual oriented. In the Islamic teachings, there is an idea that the rich should give to the poor. This is well reflected in paternalism adopted by Indonesian companies, in which the employer is expected to support the entire life of its employees and their families. Typically the Japanese company also concerns itself with the private life of its employees as well as their performance at work. However, there are notable differences between the two countries [3]. In the Japanese-style paternalism, employees do not actively pursue the right to receive assistance from the employer. If anyone gets it, it is understood that he will somehow try to pay back. Such give-and-take collectivity-oriented paternalism in Japan is used to diffuse human relationships within the group. By contrast, the Indonesian-style paternalism is very much one-sided; it makes a presupposition out of the understanding that it is natural for employees (the poor) to receive any amount of assistance from their employer (the rich). In other words, employees claim the right to receive assistance and feel nothing unusual about receiving it. This rather individual-oriented paternalism is largely used to link people through assistance handed out from above.

THE HEIR OF ANCIENT CHINA

As discussed in Chapter Four, entirely or predominantly Chinese societies such as Taiwan, Hong Kong, and Singapore are clustered very closely to one another in terms of managerial and workforce values (see Figure 4-1). The view of culture as fundamentally a cognitive system sees it as being in the same realm as language. Just as there are many different spoken Chinese languages (e.g. Mandarin, Cantonese, Shanghainese), there are subdivisions even within Chinese culture. Yet, despite the diversity in spoken languages, the Chinese have long been held together by a common written language, that has hardly changed since the early Christian era. The written Chinese language has, to a large degree, helped preserve uniquely Chinese culture not only in mainland China but also in half a dozen countries in Southeast Asia where many overseas Chinese reside.

No matter where the Chinese live, they seem to retain their own traditional values which make them quite unlike anyone else. Calling them the most paradoxical race in the world, British journalist Bonavia has remarked that the Chinese are admirable, infuriating, humorous, priggish, modest, overweening, mendacious, loyal, mercenary, ethereal, sadistic and tender; they are quite unlike anyone else [4]. The paradoxical nature of the Chinese might be illustrated by a Chinese vision of leadership as recorded in

"The Way of Lao Tzu" - a Chinese classic written in the 6th century BC:

> I have three treasures.
> Guard and keep them.
> The first is deep love.
> The second is frugality.
> And the third is not to
> dare to be ahead of the world.
> Because of deep love, one is courageous.
> Because of frugality, one is generous.
> Because of not daring to be ahead of the
> world, one becomes the leader of the world.

Chinese society has not been unchanging nor static nor inert. On the contrary, there have been continual change and great variety, but always within the limits of a distinctive cultural pattern. The Chinese cultural tradition can be traced to Confucianism, which is the faith or system of thoughts taught by Confucius (551? - 479BC) - the greatest of the sages of China. It is a rule of life rather than a religion in the Western sense of the word. More than 2,500 years ago, Confucius taught people how they should behave toward each other, rather than anything about God. His teaching has had tremendous influence on the values and behaviors of the Chinese. The center of his teaching is "jen", which roughly means benevolent love or duty to others. This is to be carried out in what Confucius called the "Five Relations" - those between ruler and subject, father and son, husband and wife, older brother and younger brother, and friend and friend. Confucius taught that man does not exist in a vacuum but he is inextricably bound up with his context including family, clan, and sovereign. He said, "If I am not to be a man among men, what am I to be?". That is to say, man can only define his self by relations to others and to the "Tao" (Way) which makes them all interdependent through the web of reciprocal obligations.

Next to "jen", Confucius put "li", another word of profound meaning that cannot be translated exactly. "Li" roughly refers to the rules of propriety which structure interpersonal relationships into hierarchical dualities as established in the Five Relations. Thus, every man is required to respect the hierarchical relationships and behave accordingly; the ideal result of this teaching is the true gentleman.

It may be suggested that these are the very values that have helped shape up Chinese society, that is characterized by high power distance and collectivism. The Chinese society, whether in Taiwan, Hong Kong, or Singapore, is indeed held together by a concept of the universe as organized and fixed with order. In such a cosmos, individual aspirations tend to be limited. The right to rebel against state power cannot be asserted in the name of individual freedom, but only in the name of the group by alleging that the leader has forfeited the mandate by not maintaining the social order adequately and correctly.

It cannot be denied that some of the traditional values have been modified or even forgotten by the Chinese in Hong Kong, who have been under strong Western influence during the last 145 years of British rule. Hong Kong, with a population of 6 million, is very much a cosmopolitan city-state. A very small number of non-Chinese (2 per cent of the total population) have also exerted themselves over the years in creating Hong Kong's unique blend of cultures. Still the vast majority of Chinese in Hong Kong carry with them the die hard values of Confucianism. In a survey conducted recently in Hong Kong, nearly all respondents stated that family group solidarity is important [5]. Only 9 per cent of the sample said they would not care if a member of their nuclear family had a quarrel with a nonrelative. Significantly, it was not only the middle-aged and elderly who considered the group to be of overwhelming importance, but this point of view was also the norm for young adults in Hong Kong.

Across the South China Sea, 2.5 million Singaporians share similar cultural heritages with their brethren in Hong Kong. In the early 1800s, the first Chinese junk had arrived at a tiny island of just 41 kilometers long and 22 kilometers wide, which was then sparsely populated with native Malays. Today, the Chinese constitute 77 per cent of the island republic's total population; 15 per cent are Malays, 6 per cent Indian, and 2 per cent Eurasian or European. Being a cosmopolitan city-state that had been under 120-year British colonial rule, Singapore too has created its own unique culture over the years. Whereas Hong Kong has been getting steady doses of Chinese culture through new immigrants arriving from mainland China, Singapore has been restricting the entry of foreigners, including the Chinese. As a result, the influence of traditional Chinese culture on her people might have diminished to a much larger extent than in Hong Kong. However, in recent years, the government under the leadership of Prime Minister Lee Kuan Yew, himself an ethnic Chinese, decided to introduce the teachings of Confucius in schools as a step toward strengthening Singapore's cultural unity. While English is being used as the official language for business, Mandarin (the standard Chinese spoken in mainland China and Taiwan) is now being taught as the second language. Here again, Singaporians' support and defense of the traditional Chinese values is quite clear and unmistakable.

Strong emphasis on loyalty to the group and interpersonal relationships within, as noted in Chinese societies, is also prevalent in Japan. This can, in large part, be explained by her import of Confucianism from China in the 17th century. In fact, Japan's national slogan before the Meiji Restoration of 1868 was "the Japanese Spirit plus Chinese Experience", which had naturally resulted in strong Chinese influence on Japanese culture. Her slogan had later changed to "the Japanese Spirit plus Western Technology", and the Chinese influence has somewhat faded in modern Japan. Few, if any, Chinese or Japanese today describe themselves as Confucian, but the Confucian values still permeate the thinking of virtually the entire population of Taiwan, Hong Kong, and Singapore as well as Japan. Together with people in Korea, which had been a satellite of China for several centuries, they are very much the heir of ancient China.

CULTURAL TRAITS - CHINESE AND JAPANESE

It is said that one of the central concepts of Chinese society is functionality, based on perhaps the most forthrightly materialistic value system in the history of mankind [6]. It has also been suggested that the Chinese are to an unusual extent pragmatic and empirical in a problemctic situation [7]. For example, in Sue and Kirk's comparative study of Chinese-Americans and Caucasian-Americans, the Chinese subjects scored higher on practical outlook, which is a strong tendency to evaluate ideas on the basis of their immediate practical application [8]. Like the Chinese, the Japanese also have a practical outlook. However, unlike the Chinese, who believe that action is functional and must always have a purpose (i.e. action is just a means to an end), the Japanese more often than not see action as its own reward (i.e. action is both a means and an end) and appreciate pain and even death caused in the course of action as transfiguring experience.

The similarity and difference between the two peoples might be explained by the Chinese concepts of "wen" and "wu". The Chinese believe in "wen" (the arts of peace and literate culture) and condone "wu" (brute force and conquest). According to a famous Chinese strategist Sun-Tzu, it is better to subdue an opponent by changing his attitude and inducing his compliance with the use of "wen". And the most economical way to do this is to make him realize his inferiority, so that he surrenders or at least retreats without the use of "wu" [9]. Such thought, that emphasizes the use of mind as a primary means of subduing an opponent, reflects the early Confucian values; and, in essence, a preference of "wen" to "wu" continues to be an important cultural trait of the Chinese.

The ethics and morals of Japanese tradition are closely tied to the Japanese interpretation of the Confucian values which had provided the Japanese with useful parameters for their own system of thoughts. The Japanese also believe in "wen", but not to such an extent as the Chinese do. Here, we cannot forget an important influence that Zen Buddhism has also had on the Japanese mode of action - the cultivation of a level mind in the face of peril, all the while bearing the physical pain of gruelling practice and training. The Confucian tradition of mind over body and the death-defying qualities of Zen Buddhism henceforth led to the birth of "Yamato-Damashi" (the indomitable Japanese spirit), which is still on the list of high priorities among the Japanese today. A legendary warrior/strategist of the Tokugawa era, Miyamoto Musashi, stated that: "the warrior's is the twofold Way of Pen and Sword, and he should have a taste for both Ways" [10]. In other words, he stressed the importance of vigorous training, both spiritual and physical, to create the man of peace and war all in one. This emphasis on both mind and body remains as one of the most important cultural traits of the Japanese that can perhaps distinguish them from the Chinese.

The two most fundamental characteristics of Japanese society are groupism and the vertical structural tendency. To a large degree, they could be traced to Confucian values of "jen" and "li", that explain the interdependent nature of human relations and hierarchically-structured interpersonal relationships within groups such as family, clan, and sovereign. These Confucian values are in fact deeply embedded in Japanese culture. We have already seen how the core values of Japanese culture - "ninjo" (human feeling), "amae" (dependence), "on" (favor/debt), and "giri" (mutual duty) - had helped generate the strong sense of attachment to groups and high priority to the correct observance of interpersonal relationships.

Needless to say, groupism and vertical relationships, as observed in Japan today, are not exactly the same as those found in Chinese society. However, evidence (e.g. findings from cultural cluster research) seems to suggest more similarities than differences, in value terms, between Japanese and Chinese societies. What are the implications of this for management practices in these two societies? We shall now attempt to find answers to this question.

JAPANESE AND CHINESE STYLES OF MANAGEMENT

At least on the surface, we could find a great many similarities in the practices of management within East Asian culture. For example, generally speaking, Japanese companies do not undertake long-range planning of a strategic nature, in the Western sense. This is not to say that they do not have long-range plans. The majority of them are, in fact, using long-range plans. However, the actual implementation of such plans in Japan is usually difficult largely due to inconsistent follow-up and a lack of well-formulated implementaion programs. Similarly in Hong Kong, the objectives of long-range planning also tend to be vague [11]; and the main goal of the company is growth-oriented, rather than financially-oriented as generally is the case for the Western companies. Furthermore, the mode of environmental monitoring both in both Japan and Hong Kong tends to be less active, structured, and systematic, when compared with the Western mode. However, in spite of these similarities, the deviation of practices from the premises of Western corporate planning appears to be less in the case of Chinese companies [12]. In other words, when compared with their Japanese counterparts, the behavior of Chinese managers, as observed in their corporate planning, appears to be closer to that of Western managers.

In contrast to Western countries, which emphasize individualistic egalitarianism, East Asian countries generally stress collective authority. However, when examined closely, there are important differences in the collectivity-orientation between Japanese and Chinese societies. In his book "My Peple and My Country", Lin has described the Chinese as a nation of individualists by noting that: the Chinese are family-oriented (like the Japanese), but not social-oriented (unlike the Japanese); the family mind is only a form of magnified selfishness, and team-work is almost unknown; the Chinese always say of themselves that their nation is like "a tray of loose sands", each grain being not an individual but a family; on the other hand, the Japanese nation is welded together like "a piece of granite" [13].

Western societies might be referred to as "a sand society", in which each grain is an individual. Masatsugu coined the terms "mosaic" and "blend" societies to explain the contrast between the West and Japan [14]. In a mosaic composition, each tile retains its unique shape and color while forming part of the whole; so it is in the West. The self is like a single tile in a mosaic. Each individual lives by emphasizing and expressing his uniqueness within the social order; the self is not lost. Chinese society also appears to be rather like a mosaic composition, but a family constitutes a single tile; it can only be considered collectivity-oriented in the sense that the self is lost in the name of a family. By contrast, Japan is a blend society, in which one's identity is lost by merging with a larger entity. Just as rice loses its original nature when each grain is blended to make "sake" (Japanese wine), the blending and dissolution of each individual in Japanese society produces a new social energy and activity.

Collectivity-orientation, generally found in both Japanese and Chinese societies, is discerned as the acceptance of the group norms as one's own values. The individual thus aspires to attach himself to a group and firmly establish himself within that group. In Japan, such a value orientation prevails in a traditional household of related members as well as in an artificial or simulated kinship group of unrelated individuals (e.g. business enterprises). On the other hand, the Chinese orientation is one of the clan-type collectivity. The clan is the close sociological, economical, and formal relationships amongst those members, who are mutually united by common ancestry, common name, common property, marriage, and shared understanding of the particularistic world view. For the Chinese, only the members of the clan can be trusted, and the nation, government, army, police, law and society are nothing but fabrication [15]. In their view, the interior world is completely separated from the exterior world; and the collectivity-orientation, that prevails within the clan, is often replaced by the individual-orientation at the outside workplace.

A comparative study of Japanese and Chinese organization structures by Redding and Pugh pointed out that Hong Kong organizations are distinctively less formalized than the Western, and Japanese distinctively more. The large disparity indicates that the Chinese and Japanese organize very differently, displaying more variations between them than between either of them and the West [16]. The finding was founded on a comparative analysis of data collected from 53 Chinese owned and managed companies in Hong Kong, using the Aston instrument, and those from Japanese and UK companies stored in the Aston data bank [17]. In 33 out of the 38 scales they used to measure the overall formalization, the scoring was simply based on whether the activity enquired about took place or not. In the Japanese case, these activities were mostly present, whereas in the Chinese case they mostly did not take place at all. Table 5-1 makes the point clear by giving some examples. In the main, Redding and Pugh's study found that:

* Aspects of basic design of the organization, such as written policies, operating instructions, job descriptions and manuals, display major Chinese/Japanese differences - especially low level in the Chinese case.
* Aspects of workflow itself, such as production schedules, recording direct workers' time, documenting work done, and minutes and agendas for executive meetings, show much closer similarity.
* Aspects of general administration, only indirectly related to workflow, such as written research and conference reports, work assessment records, and welfare documents, also show quite strong but not extreme differences.

Table 5-1: Scoring on Overall Formalization
- Hong Kong vs. Japan

	Hong Kong	Japan
	Present/Absent	Present/Absent
Written Policies	14/39	40/8
Written Operating Instructions	13/40	39/10
Manuals of Procedure	10/43	41/7
Written Research Programs/Reports	15/38	38/10
Conference Reports	15/38	39/9
Work Assessment Records	15/38	40/8
Welfare Documents	19/34	36/12

[Adapted from Redding, S.G. and D.S. Pugh, 1986, pp.163-164]

In explaining major differences between the Japanese and Chinese companies, they suggested that the high level of formalization in Japanese organizations was suited to a culture with high expectations about the formalization of social process. In the case of Hong Kong, somehow the Confucian disciplines, which reinforce hierarchies in Chinese organizations, removed the need for measures to formalize processes of cooperation. Quite possibly, the variation could also be explained by the fact that the Chinese norms are the small-scale family business where the clan-type collectivity prevails, whereas the Japanese norms are the large-scale enterprises where the family-type collectivity, based on the concept of "ie" (household), prevails. However, Redding and Pugh noted that the cultural influences on the organizations were independent of the imperatives of the size/structure relationships.

By far the most significant difference between the Japanese and Chinese could be found in their leadership patterns, as perhaps best reflected in managerial decision-making. Silin's study of large-scale enterprises in Taiwan, for example, has suggested that while Chinese and Japanese enterprises superficially share many formal structural elements, they are differentiated largely on the basis of variations in the relationships between superiors and subordinates [18]. The Chinese pattern of leadership emphasizes rational commitment to the leader, rather than emotional ties as generally found in Japan. Therefore, any attempts at creating a more informal affective atmosphere on the part of subordinates, especially those who do not belong to the clan, are interpreted by Chinese leaders as efforts to undercut leaders' prerogatives. Chinese leaders thus maintain considerable distance in their relations with subordinates by suppressing close inclinations on the part of subordinates. Unlike Japanese leaders who admit their dependence on subordinates, Chinese leaders attempt to achieve goals through fostering competition among subordinates. They tend to play down or even deny the contribution of subordiantes and often play off various subgroups within the organization through divide-and-rule tactics, which are rarely employed by Japanese leaders.

Japanese leaders' emphasis on emotional ties and their dependence on subordinates could be explained, to a considerable degree, by two of the core values of Japanese culture - "ninjo" (human feeling) and "amae" (dependence). These values are generally absent in Chinese society, except within the clan-type collectivity. One of the central concepts of Chinese society is functionality. Whereas the Japanese generally believe that action is both a means and an end, the Chinese believe that action is merely a means to an end. There seems to exist within the Chinese enterprise an inner tension. The pervasive ambition for individuals to strike out on their own tends to deny the Chinese leader of dependable subordinates; the loyalty of subordinates is not taken for granted, especially in large enterprises which have grown out of the small-scale family business. The maintenance of tight personal control over all areas of management, a low degree of delegation of authority, an autocratic approach in their interpersonal dealings with subordinates, and a highly personalized style of leadership are some of the main characteristics of Chinese management [19].

The formal rejection of the affective component in personal relations has direct implications for the managerial decision-making style of Chinese management. Japanese leaders generally believe that changes and initiatives within the organization must come from those closest to problems, and act primarily as the facilitator of decision-making. By contrast, Chinese leaders tend to assume responsibility for all decisions and relinquish little of thier authority except operating decisions; they act as the real decison-maker. In this sense, then, we can say that the decision-making behavior of Chinese managers is rather like that of Western managers. Pye and Solomon suggested a picture of Chinese as passive and as preferring that others make decisions for them [20]. Chinese subordinates prefer to be in a situation in which the leader provides guidance and takes responsibility for determining a proper course of action. This is in sharp contrast to the Japanese case, where subordinates are encouraged and are also willing to take initiatives in decision-making. A similar observation was made by Woronoff who said, "When our two Asian brethren get together for business, they are liable to encounter some little difficulty if they foolishly assume they are brothers under the skin and will react in the same way; for, if he is not careful, the Chinese boss - the man with all the power and who can make snap decisions - will be meeting with a purely ceremonial (Japanese) boss who at best can freely decide which restaurant they should dine at." [21]

The Japanese company could be viewed as a combination of average leadership and able and motivated masses. Employees at middle and lower echelons are said to be highly motivated to fully exercise their potentials. In other words, the gap in motivation is relatively small in Japan partly because the top executives seldom monopolize information about the organization; the sense of participation is stronger at lower levels compared with foreign organizations, including the Chinese, where one generally sees a combination of high-caliber leaders and less competent masses [22].

CHINESE FIRM IN HONG KONG - A CASE STUDY

In explaining the philosophy of the company he had co-founded, Akio Morita said, "People of SONY always unite harmoniously and closely because of the joy of participating in creative work and their pride in contributing their own unique talents to this aim." [23]. "Wa" (harmony) is considered most important in the company's family-like cohesive environment. If anyone violates the harmony of the group by selling himself too hard, he will be excluded from the group. In other words, nobody can be a star in the Japanese company. Similarly in a speech delivered at a management seminar, the Managing Director of a leading construction company, owned and run by the Chinese in Hong Kong, also stressed the importance of collective efforts and team-work. He said, "Think about the soccer team. It is easy for the goal-scorer to become a hero. But if there is no defence in the backs, the team can still lose the match. Team effort is more important than heroism ... So it is with a management team."

Despite this similarity in the management philosophy, a close look at this Chinese firm in Hong Kong has produced strong evidence that the

Chinese are indeed different from the Japanese in decision-making style. When asked to explain the process used for making important decisions, the Executive Director of the company, Mr. Chan, remarked:

> "We make almost all major decisions together at meetings. So we cannot really place responsibility on any particular individual. When something goes wrong, we get together again, discuss the problem, and try to find a way out. Our emphasis is on team-work. Of course, if someone does an exceptionally good job, we give him an extra bonus at the year-end. But even that is not so much more than what everbody else in the team gets."

This remark suggests that the nature of the decison-making process adopted at the firm is collective; and, in fact, important decisions are made collectively at regular meetings such as:

* Bi-weekly senior management meetings attended by the Managing Director, the Executive Director and the Department Heads.
* Bi-weekly management meetings attended by the Executive Directors and the Department Heads.
* Monthly departmental meetings attended by the Department Head and all senior staff in the Department.

Much like their Japanese counterparts, the firm's managers believe that subordinates should be encouraged and allowed to participate in decision-making. Mr. Chan, for example, typically instructs his subordinates to work out several alternative proposals among themselves first before submitting one final proposal to him for further discussions at the bi-weekly management meeting, which he chairs himself. He stated his personal involvement in decision-making as follows:

> "Once I give out my instructions, I try not to get involved in the initial preparation of alternative proposals. I only drop in at their meetings occasionally to give my own piece of mind and additional guidelines. In any

case, I ask for the minutes of all
meetings held by my subordinates.
Besides, I don't just look at the final
conclusion. Our company is still young
(10 years old), and it is very important
for me to check the validity of raw data
and information submitted to me together
with one final proposal."

Such an extent of his personal involvement at the
initial stage of decision-making as well as a
close scrutinization of the final proposal
suggests that little room for initiatives is
actually left to subordinates and a wide range of
activities is subtly but surely controlled by the
leader. Although an important decision may
appear to be made through the bottom-up process,
it is more often than not reached under a strong
and continual influence from the higher levels.
On the basis of this observation, perhaps the
firm's decision-making process could be more
accurately described as one of top-down approach.

In principle, the managers of this Hong Kong
Chinese company all believe in team-work and
collective efforts much like Japanese managers.
Yet, in reality, the company's decison-making
process does not seem very collective, either.
Perhaps the best indicator of a general awareness
that decisions are made collectively is a
thorough dissemination of information within the
organization. In his study of Japanese
companies, Clark has noted that dozens of
documents seem to be in circulation, so that
company members know a great deal of what is
going on, even if it scarcely concerns them [24].

Besides the circulation of numerous formal
documents, Japanese companies typically use
various informal channels of communication, such
as "nemawashi" at the work-place and off-hour
drinking sessions, to achieve the free flow of
information. By contrast, the Chinese company
under study relies almost solely on the formal
channels of communication for the exchange of
information and tends to neglect the use of
informal channels of communication. For example,
although informal discussions and consultations
take place frequently at the workplace, managers
seldom go out with their subordinates outside the
working-hour for casual drinks and meals, which

could be very useful to enhance the team spirit and togetherness. When they do, they usually get together only with the peers of the same or similar ranks. However, even on such occasions, they seem to talk very little about personal matters. Mr. Lam, one of the Department Heads directly reporting to the Executive Director confessed:

> "We feel the pressure of work 24 hours a day, and we cannot even relax when we are supposed to be having fun together. We always end up talking about work. It never occurred to me that I was so involved with the company business until my wife angrily complained, 'Don't you people have anything else to talk about? I was bored stiff!', after one recent company dinner party which we had both attended."

Furthermore, the effectiveness of their formal channels of communication is somewhat questionable. Whereas the official minutes of meetings and the like are widely circulated horizontally across departments as well as vertically across management levels, managers show a very high degree of reluctance to reveal any matters that they consider as no direct concern of others. Mr. Lam confided:

> "By reading all those minutes of meetings, I think I know what is going on even outside my own department. I want to believe that people here are quite open in communication. But honestly, I am not sure how much information they are giving away ... Earlier this year, we had a fire at one of our construction sites, but nobody bothered to inform the Managing Director. It was put out quickly, and I myself did not know anything about it. That same evening, we had a dinner party and somehow the boss found that out. You can imagine how mad he was."

Mr. Lau's colleague of the same rank explained:

"If any big problem comes up, we immediately set up an ad hoc committee to
put out a fire by ourselves. Then it is
all up to me to decide whether or not we
should refer the matter to anyone else.
In most cases, we can manage to find a
solution ourselves without bothering
anyone outside the department."

On these grounds, it is rather doubtful if the
decision-making process adopted in this Chinese
company could be regarded as collective, at least
in the Japanese sense.

DIFFERENCES AMID SIMILARITIES IN EAST ASIA

Mun's exploratory study of manufacturing
enterprises in mainland China (PRC) has indicated
that though operating under an entirely
different political and economic system, the
characteristics of the PRC's management resemble,
to a significant degree, those generally found in
other Chinese societies such as Hong Kong and
Taiwan [25]. For example, the authoritative
approach to decision-making is closer to the
American, but the collective responsibility for
decisions in the PRC makes it closer to the
Japanese. Table 5-2 shows the classification of
decision-making style into four types.

Table 5-2: Four Styles of Decision-making

Responsibility for Decisions	Decision-making Approach	
	Authoritative	Participative
Individual	"Type A": American-style	"Type Z": Mixture of A & J
Collective	"Type C": Chinese-style	"Type J": Japanese-style

[Adapted from Mun, K.C., 1986, p.325]

119

It must be noted, however, that the characteristics of Chinese management in the PRC are fast
changing due to the on-going economic and
management reforms. Since 1979 when the current
political leaders came to power, the PRC's
government has been increasingly emphasizing
autonomy and economic accountability for its
enterprises. Mun's study has pointed to a
shifting preference among Chinese managers in the
PRC toward a more participative approach to
decision-making and an individual responsibility
system (i.e. Type Z Management). Chinese
scholars are of the opinion that their
enterprises should develop their own style of
decision-making in order to meet the specific
conditions of the PRC.

In the same vein, a comparative study of
Japanese, Korean and American managerial
decision-making styles conducted by Oh and
Boulgarides has indicated that the Japanese and
Korean styles are similar but not exactly the
same [26]. The cognitive-contingency decision
style model proposed by these two researchers,

Table 5-3: The Cognitive-Contingency Decision
Style Model

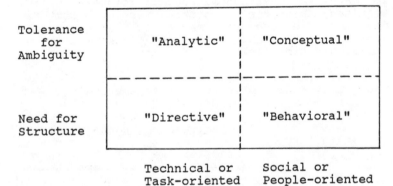

Tolerance for Ambiguity	"Analytic"	"Conceptual"
Need for Structure	"Directive"	"Behavioral"
	Technical or Task-oriented	Social or People-oriented

[Adapted from Boulgarides, J.D.. and M.D. Oh,
1985, p.9]

shown in Table 5-3, classifies individual decision-makers into four types - directive, analytic, conceptual, and behavioral. The vertical dimension of the model deals with the way individuals perceive the environment surrounding them. The low cognitively complex individuals tend to perceive the environment in terms of few rigid rules of information processing and have a high need for structure; they generally focus on short-range goals and use limited information in arriving at decisions. By contrast, the high cognitively complex individuals have a high tolerance for ambiguity and use condiderable information in arriving at decisions which focus on long-range goals.

The horizontal dimension of the model deals with the environment confronting individuals and their reaction to differences between the perceived and internalized view of the environment. The left half of the model corresponds with those individuals who generally prefer technical or task-oriented environments; they tend to be narrowly-focused, logical or analytical thinkers and prefer written reports to face-to-face meetings. On the other hand, those individuals falling in the right half prefer social or people-oriented environments; they tend to think in broad or spatial terms and prefer meetings to written reports. Comparing the three national samples, the two researchers concluded that:

* Americans are most directive and analytic of the three but least conceptual and behavioral.
* Japanese are least directive and analytic but most conceptual and behavioral of the three.
* Koreans fall between the American and Japanese samples for each of the four decision-making styles.

They also noted that as a whole, the Japanese and Korean samples were more alike and, in fact, different from the American sample in the sense that they are people rather than task oriented in their approach to decision-making.

To sum up, cultural differences have led to diversities in the practices of management around the world, as clearly seen in sharp contrasts between East and West, and even among countries in East Asia. The influence of culture, embedded in a society, is quite considerable. The

Japanese, the Chinese and the Koreans share a common value system, as codified in ancient Confucianism, and they appear to have more similarities than differences in their practices of management. However, even these heirs of Confucianism have given different interpretations to the original Confucian values and modified them to meet their own specific conditions over the centuries. It is quite clear that though a common cultural heritage from the past has no doubt contributed to making their practices similar in many aspects, it has not been powerful enough to make them exactly the same.

Notes

1. Ichikawa, K., "Opportunism and National Characteristics of Thai People", Sociopsychology Annual Report ('Nempo Shakai Shinrigaku', 1986), pp.14-34

2. Hanada, M., "A Cross-Cultural Comparison of Work Attitudes and Behavior", mimeograph, Tokyo: Human Development Center, (Apr. 1984)

3. ibid.

4. Bonavia, D., The Chinese, London: Allen Lane, (1981)

5. Lau, S.K., Society and Politics in Hong Kong, Chinese University of Hong Kong Press, (1982)

6. Bonavia, D., (1981), op.cit.

7. Freeman, R., "Overview" in Cho and Kobayashi (eds.), Fertility Transition of the East Asia Populations, Honolulu: University of Hawaii Press, (1979)

8. Sue, D.W. and B.A. Kirk, "Psychological Characteristics of Chinese-American Students", Journal of Counseling Psychology, (1972), vol. 19, pp.471-478

9. Sun Tzu, The Art of War, Griffith, S.B. (trans.), London: Oxford University Press, (1963)

10. Miyamoto Musashi, A Book of Five Rings, Harris, V. (trans.), Woodstock, NY: The Overlook Press, (1974)

11. Lau, H.F. and M.K. Nyaw, "Management Practices of Hong Kong Chinese Translational Companies: An Exploratory Study", Proceedings of the Academy of International Business (Southeast Asian region) Conference, (Jul. 1985), pp.441-550

12. Fukuda, K.J., "Japanese and Chinese Management Information Systems and the Question of Transferability", Ph.D. thesis, University of Hong Kong, (1982)

13. Lin, Y.T., My Country and My People, London: Heinemann, (1962)

14. Masatsugu, M., Management and Society: Lessons from Contemporary Japan, Singapore: Federal Publications, (1985)

15. Nakayama, I., "How to Deal with Overseas Chinese", mimeograph, Singapore: Japanese Chamber of Commerce and Industry, (1980)

16. Redding, S.G. and D.S. Pugh, "The Formal and the Informal: Japanese and Chinese Organization Structures", in S.R. Clegg, D.C. Dunphy, and S.G. Redding (eds.), The Enterprise and Management in East Asia, Hong Kong: Center of Asian Studies, (1986), pp.153-167

17. Dickson, D.J. and C.J. McMillan, Organization and Nation: the Aston Program IV, Farnborough, Hampshire: Gower Publishing Co., (1971)

18. Silin, R.H., Leadership and Values: The Organization of Large-Scale Taiwanese Enterprises, Cambridge, MA: Harvard University Press, (1976)

19. Lau, H.F. and M.K. Nyaw, (1985), op.cit. Silin, R.H., (1976), op.cit.

20. Pye, L.W., The Spirit of Chinese Politics, Cambridge, MA: MIT Press, (1968); Solomon, R.H., Mao's Revolution and the Chinese Political Culture, Berkeley: University of California Press, (1971)

21. Woronoff, J., "Cultures Collide in East to East Trade", Asian Business, (Apr. 1980), pp.50-53

22. Ishida, H., "Transferability of Japanese Human Resource Management Abroad", Human Resource Management, (Spring 1986), pp.103-120

23. Morita, A., Made in Japan, London: Collins, (1987), p.147

24. Clark, R., The Japanese Company, New Haven: Yale University Press, (1979)

25. Mun, K.C., "Characteristics of the Chinese Management: An Exploratory Study", in S.R. Clegg, D.C. Dunphy, and S.G. Redding (eds.), <u>The Enterprise and Management in East Asia</u>, Hong Kong: Center of Asian Studies, (1986), pp.313-326

26. Boulgarides, J.D. and M.D. Oh, "A Comparison of Japanese, Korean and American Managerial Decision Styles: An Exploratory Study", <u>Leadership and Organization Development Journal</u>, (1985), vo.6, no.1, pp.9-11

Chapter Six

JAPANESE-STYLE MANAGEMENT: HOW MUCH IS IT
PRACTICED ABROAD?

Japan's recent climb to the top spot as the
world's most competitive nation in business could
well be explained by the effectiveness of
management as practiced in the home country. As
Japan's direct investments overseas keep on
growing at a phenomenal rate, the home-grown
practices of Japanese-style management are also
being exported abroad by an increasing number of
Japanese companies which are setting up or
expanding their overseas operations. Can the
features, unique to Japanese management, be
successfully transferred abroad to realize the
same sort of management effectiveness that has
been achieved at home? As a step toward
obtaining an answer to this question, it may be
useful to find out how much (or how little) of
Japanese-style management is actually practiced
outside Japan. This chapter presents findings
from a survey conducted to examine the extent to
which some of the most distinctive features of
Japanese-style management are employed by
Japanese companies operating in two predominantly
Chinese city-states, Hong Kong and Singapore. In
addition, findings from the identical survey
conducted among Hong Kong's local companies are
also presented in order to uncover similarities
and differences in the practices of management
across nations as well as cultures.

SWEET AND SOUR TASTE OF SUCCESS

"Japan is the rich neighbor everyone loves to
hate", proclaimed FORTUNE International,
describing the accomplishment of its World War II
goal of a "Greater East Asia Co-Prosperity
Sphere" [1]. As the country's economic might
grows, the Japanese are encountering a love-hate
reaction from their Asian neighbors. Japan is

finding that its ascent to the ranks of economic super-power brings not only high praises but also relentless criticisms. Especially in East Asia, those sensitive to Japan's military past now worry about its economic domination. The main criticisms most often raised by the Asian neighbors are:

* Japan floods their market with Japanese goods, while its barriers to foreign-made goods fuel chronic trade deficits.
* Japanese investment is welcome, but Japanese companies simply take advantages of cheap labor without sharing the technology needed by developing countries.
* The Japanese are often too oblivious of Asian sentiment; they appear aloof and insensitive to the aspirations of their neighbors.

Still, for all their resentment, the neighbors envy Japan's achievement; and several countries in the region such as Singapore and Malaysia have long pursued a "Look East" policy that seeks to emulate Japan's economic miracle in the Post-War period. East Asian countries, which objected to a Japanese business presence only a decade ago, are now actively seeking investment from Japan. Some have stepped up the drive to attract more Japanese direct investment mainly to create new jobs and thus alleviate the serious unemployment problem. Japanese investment is sorely needed in countries such as Indonesia, which must create 1.6 million new jobs a year, or Thailand and the Philippines where 700,000 more people must find work each year. Though they have achieved their own economic mini-miracles, Asia's four newly-industrialized nations (NICs) are equally eager to get a lion's share of Japanese overseas investment, more for obtaining advanced technology much needed in their countries than for merely creating new jobs. All in all, by the end of the fiscal year which ended on March 31, 1987, cumulative Japanese direct investment in East Asia reached US$21.8 billion, or 20.6 per cent of the country's total direct investments overseas - second only to North America whose share was 35.5 per cent [2].

Since the signing of the historic agreement in 1984 between the UK and China on the future of Hong Kong, a new wave of Japanese companies has been arriving in Hong Kong, with long-term commitment beyond 1997 - the year China will regain its sovereignty over Hong Kong - to capitalize on the new-found political stability in this outpost of China. As of March 31, 1986, Hong Kong was the world's seventh most popular destination for Japanese direct investment, with $2.9 billion on a cumulative basis. Singapore, the smallest of the four Asian NICs (population 2.6 million), has also seen the rapid growth of Japanese investment in recent years. Japan's direct investment in the country doubled in 1986 to around $230 million. Similarly, Japanese investment in Taiwan rose to $151 million in the first five months of 1987 from $81 million in the previous year. In the same period, South Korea also approved $150 million worth of Japanese investment, compared with $35 million a year earlier.

In addition to effects on a recipient country's local employment through the establishment of factories and branch offices or industrial development through the transfer of technology, direct investment contributes to the country's foreign exchange position through substituting imports with expanded domestic production capacities. As shown in Table 6-1, Japan's direct investment overseas can be classified into four types by objectives: resource-seeking, import-substituting, export-oriented and service-sector [3].

Of the four types of investment, the first two were predominant up to the first investment boom in 1972-73. Most of the investments, small in scale, went to resource-endowed or low-wage countries in East Asia and South America. Then in the second boom period that began in the early 1980s, the Japanese investment shifted into the US and Western European countries, where the investment was mostly import-substituting. In this period, Japanese investment in East Asia and South America grew only at a moderate speed, resulting in a diminished share for these areas.

Table 6-1: Classification of Japan's Direct
          Overseas Investment

Resource-seeking	Aims at seeking natural resources overseas to be imported for processing in Japan.
Import-substituting Investment	Aims at substituting imports, from Japan to a recipient country, with goods manufactured in that country.
Export-oriented Investment	Aims at exporting goods manufactured in a recipient country to third countries.
Service-sector Investment	Aims at providing business services (e.g. banking, retailing) in a recipient country.

In the mid-1980s, Japan entered the third boom period for overseas investment. While the pace of import-substituting investment into developed countries in the West has accelerated, the export-oriented type of investment has begun to rush to East Asian and other developing countries. Furthermore, this period has seen a sharp increase in investment in the service sector, as being observed in countries with well-developed financial, property and retail markets. The resource-seeking and import-substituting investments are still predominant in Indonesia, the biggest recipient of Japan's direct investment in East Asia; but most of Japanese companies operating today in Asia's NICs are in either export-oriented manufacturing industries or the service sector.

In short, the internationalization of Japanese business, driven by rapidly expanding direct overseas investment, has gone through three stages of development over the last 30 years or so:

Stage I   - Export of goods manufactured in Japan, using raw materials imported from developing countries.
Stage II - Overseas production in a country, which has been the export market for goods made in Japan.

Stage III - Overseas production in a country for export to third countries, coupled with expansion in the provision of business services.

The strong yen, standing at 125 to the US dollar (as of December 1987) compared with more than 200 two years earlier, has made goods produced in Japan less competitive in foreign markets. As a result, hard-pressed Japanese manufacturers are pouring investment capital around East Asia to boost production overseas and deflect steep rises in cost at home. The recent rush of export-oriented investment is only the beginning. The majority of Japanese companies are still at the second stage (i.e. import-substituting type of operation), and only a handful of them has so far reached the third stage (i.e. export-oriented type of operations). It may, therefore, be quite some time before many will reach the next stage, in which broader management strategies are developed on a global basis as is the case of the long-established multinationals such as IBM and Shell. Heavily loaded with the surplus capital at present, Japan's direct overseas investment still has a great deal of potential for growth. Compared with other industrialized countries in the West, its per capita amount is only one-third of that of the US and one-half of West Germany. Of the cumulative total of 8,123 foreign investments in the US for 1974-85, Japan was behind Canada and the UK, with 1,154 investments [4]. The Ministry of Industry and Trade forecast that by 1993, goods produced by Japanese companies abroad would equal 8.3 per cent of Japan's GNP, compared with 4.2 per cent in 1984. It is also estimated that some 30 to 40 per cent of the total would be from factories in East Asia.

Japanese businesses have just begun to internationalize their operations on a large scale, and this process is expected to move at an accelerated pace. In the process of becoming truly internationalized multinationals, there is no way that Japanese companies can leave behind what they have known and done at home for so many years. When venturing out of Japan's insular society, they necessarily take along the features of their own style of management which are deeply rooted in Japan's cultural traditions. Japanese managers are accustomed to their home country

workers who can work harmoniously in groups, find
the meaning of work themselves, and willingly
play an active role in the management process.
Japanese workers are also long used to the
life-time employment system, which strips away a
great deal of personal freedom, or the seniority
system which calls for much patience in getting
promotion. Inevitably, situations in host
countries that Japanese managers must face up to,
such as the work ethic of employees and the local
business and management practices, are not the
same as those which have been taken almost for
granted at home.

"IN ROME, DO AS THE ROMANS DO"

We have already examined in some detail several
features that make traditional Japanese management distinct from Western management. Briefly,
they are:

* Group-orientation (Emphasis on group harmony)
* Community-orientation (Total concern for
  people)
* Group, rather than individual, duties and
  responsibilities (Focus on human relations in
  groups, rather than functional relationships)
* Life-time employment system (Job security for
  employees and loyalty to the company)
* Seniority-based pay and promotion system
  (Rewards for long-serving employees)
* Continuous and extensive on-the-job training
  (Development of employees' skills useful for
  the company)
* Frequent job rotation (Development of the
  generalist)

Important questions that need to be addressed
now are: which of these features have Japanese
companies attempted to export abroad, and what is
the outcome of their efforts to date? There is
some evidence that the well-intended employment
of certain features has not been received with
much enthusiasm by non-Japanese employees abroad
[5]. For example, the practice of visiting sick
employees at home, in line with the general
thrust of community-oriented management ideology,
had to be abandoned by some Japanese companies in
the UK because it was perceived by local
employees as a means to control absenteeism

rather than a genuine concern for the employees' well-being. A survey of Japanese manufacturing subsidiaries operating in Europe, which was carried out in 1985 by Japan External Trade Organization, showed that few of the companies had tried to export Japanese management practices wholesale but primarily chosen to adapt to local conditions. Although many of the companies studies reported success in transplanting certain features of Japanese-style management and improving both labor productivity and product quality, the study indicated the difficulty in introducing onto the European soil such practices as fusing the interests of management and labor. For example, in explaining labor conditions in Europe, it noted that European workers did not consider work to be the center of their lives, but considered it as something that they had to do to live. By contrast, Japanese workers typically have a strong inner urge to work; they take pride in their work; they do not feel exploited by the company; they almost seem to "live to work". There surely lies the difficulty in expecting European workers to contribute or stay loyal to the company to the same extent as Japanese workers do.

A study of Japanese subsidiaries in the UK pointed out that: if "Japaneseness" is measured by the degree of home country managerial practices introduced, then the short answer is that a minority of firms are quite "Japanese", and a small number quite "British"; the majority are managed according to ad hoc compromise, without any definite plan to determine what best practice in the circumstances might be, and they range along a continuum between the two hypothetical poles [6]. The study's major findings included:

* The introduction of Japanese values of group cohesion has been attempted but largely failed in the face of British values of individualism, resulting in the difficulty of implant team work.
* Total concern for people, another important value typically held by Japanese companies, is not an empty slogan. It is widely adopted by Japanese companies operating in the UK.

* The benefits of the life-time employment system
  are not available to local employees, who are
  recruited under different conditions as
  non-permanent staff.
* Local employees' pay, promotion, and other
  benefits are separately administered from those
  of Japanese expatriates. However, many enjoy
  attractive benefits such as pension schemes,
  low cost loans and private health insurance
  once they have served a minimum number of
  years.
* The British system of functional specialization and the structure of individual careers,
  across different organizations, has made it
  hard, if not impossible, to introduce job
  rotation and on-the-job training.

"In Rome, do as the Romans do", say Japanese
executives who have had the experience of running
their companies' subsidiaries in the US. Many of
them have spoken out of the danger involved in
pushing on American workers certain features of
Japanese-style management such as group
activities, the seniority-based pay/promotion
system and the life-time employment system.
Still, among the overwhelming majority of these
Japanese executives, there appears to be a strong
consensus regarding the importance of implanting
the corporate ideologies of goup-orientation and
community-orientation.

Kyocera Corporation, a major computer-chip
maker, is one such company that firmly believes
in the merit of introducing these ideologies even
to American soil [7]. At first, the company
refrained from forcing Kyoceraism on American
workers. However, seeing that labor-management
relations did not improve, the president sent to
the US subsidiary instructions to push through
with the Kyocera way without being afraid of the
consequences. Kyocera's American president was
dismissed; the Japanese came to the front and
started to build up human relations in the way
they knew best, e.g. morning physical exercises
and pep talk, after-work get-togethers for a
drink, same dining hall for executives and
rank-and-file workers. This has created among
local employees the family-like feeling of
oneness with the management. Today, having
adopted even the life-time employment system in
their US subsidiary, the company's Japanese
executives never fail to stress to job applicants

that loyalty to the company is one of the conditions for employment.

Perhaps, Kyocera is an extreme case. But there are numerous other cases in which Japanese companies operating in the US have succeeded in transplanting Japanese-style management by emphasizing group harmony and respect for human dignity. They have introduced small yet very innovative Japanese ways to cultivate a sense of oneness with the company and demonstrate their total concern for each and every individual. While the active learning process and bold experiments continue, the vast majority of Japanese companies in Europe or the US have not come to the point of employing all the features of Japanese-style management. Obviously, being only too aware of cultural differences between the East and the West, they have instead chosen to adapt to local conditions.

"IN ASIA, DO AS THE JAPANESE DO?"

Let us now turn our attention to East Asia and examine what Japanese companies have attempted and achieved in transplanting traditional Japanese management on Asian soil. Many Japanese managers stationed in the region tend to think that a geographical proximity and cultural similarity will automatically make their local Asian employees think and behave very much like themselves. Some of them, sometimes suffering from a superiority complex toward fellow Asians, even feel that their local employees must think and behave like the Japanese.

Hong Kong and Singapore have attracted a large sum of Japanese direct investment during the past two decades. They also occupy the top two positions among Asia's NICs in terms of per capita GNP (US$6,173 and $7,200, respectively). Furthermore, unlike most other countries, the governments of Hong Kong or Singapore impose practically no conditions and restrictions on foreign investors, enabling them to run their businesses almost as freely as they wish. Therefore, they may be considered as the ideal places to conduct a study to determine the transferability of Japanese-style management abroad.

As a step toward achieving this goal, a mailed questionnaire survey of Japanese subsidiaries in Hong Kong and Singapore was conducted, with the aim of finding out how much (or how little) of the features of Japanese-style management has actually been introduced. Findings from the survey of these two groups of companies, with the same cultural origin but operating in different locations, will enable us to do a cross-national comparison of management. In addition, an identical survey of the leading local companies in Hong Kong was carried out. These local companies and Japanese subsidiaries in Hong Kong operate in the same location, but they are of different cultural origins. Findings from this additional survey will, therefore, be used to conduct a cross-cultural comparative analysis of management.

One hundred and twenty-five Japanese subsidiaries in Hong Kong were selected from the Directory of Corporate Members, published in 1986 by the Hong Kong Japanese Club. At the end, 67 of them agreed to participate in the survey by returning the completed questionnaires. This represented around 8.5 per cent of the total number of Japanese companies operating in Hong Kong. The sample companies ranged from a large department store established in 1960, with over 700 employees, to a bank opened in 1984, with 30 employees. Most of these subsidiaries were established in Hong Kong either in the 1960s (30 per cent) or in the 1970s (40 per cent). On the average, the sample company had 11 Japanese and 140 local Hong Kong employees on its payroll.

Using the similar directory published in 1986 by the Japanese Association of Singapore, 101 Japanese subsidiaries in Singapore were also contacted. After the second mailing of survey questionnaires, 43 companies sent back the completed questionnaires. Like in Hong Kong, this represented some 8.5 per cent of the total number of Japanese companies operating in Singapore. Though two of these companies (a bank and a trading house) started their operation in Singapore in the mid-1950s, the great majority of them (67 per cent) were established in the 1970s. The average numbers of Japanese and local employees among the sample companies were 16 and 164, respectively.

Of the 70 Hong Kong local companies selected for the survey, 38 returned the completed questionnaires. This represented about 16 per cent of the total number of companies publicly listed in the Hong Kong Stock Exchange. They ranged from a major bank with more than 11,000 employees to a property development company with about 80 employees (average number 1,900). Except for 6 "hongs" (long-established conglomerates run mostly by British expatriates), the sample companies are owned and managed by the local Chinese. Table 6-2 shows the breakdown of the selected companies by industry.

Table 6-2: Breakdown of Sample Companies by
          Industry

	Japanese (Hong Kong)	Japanese (Singapore)	Locals (Hong Kong)
Manufacturing, Engineering, Construction	19(28%)	18(42%)	13(34%)
Import/Export, Wholesale/Retail	19(28%)	9(21%)	8(21%)
Finance, Banking	16(24%)	7(16%)	7(19%)
Others (Utility, Transportation, Tourism, Property, etc.)	13(20%)	9(21%)	10(26%)
Total	67(100%)	43(100%)	38(100%)

The survey questionnaire, mailed out to the personnel manager of each selected company, asked the respondent to indicate the degree of actual employment of given features of management at his or her own organization. The nine features included in the questionnaire were:

* Emphasis on group harmony ("Harmony")
* Total concern for people ("People")
* Collective decision-making by consensus
  ("Consensus")

* Group, rather than individual, duties and
  responsibilities ("Group")
* Life-time employment system ("Employment")
* Seniority-based pay system ("Pay")
* Seniority-based promotion system ("Promotion")
* On-the-Job training ("Training")
* Job rotation ("Rotation")

These are all regarded as the features that
make Japanese management distinct from Western
management (see Table 3-3: Features of Japanese-
style management). Comprehensive welfare programs, though a feature typically employed by
Japanese companies in Japan, were not included in
the questionnaire. It was excluded because most
companies, Japanese or non-Japanese, have welfare
programs of one sort or another and, moreover,
the understanding of "comprehensiveness" could
vary considerably in the mind of respondents.
Nevertheless, the extent of the employment of
this particular feature might be reflected in the
answer given to "total concern for people". In
the point-scale of 1 to 3, "1" indicates not
employed at all, "2" indicates somewhat employed,
and "3" indicates employed entirely. Figure 6-1
shows the mean scores obtained by three different
groups of sample companies.
It can be seen that the feature employed the
most by the Japanese companies in both Hong Kong
and Singapore is "emphasis on group harmony", 58
per cent and 47 per cent of the companies
surveyed respectively stating that it is employed
entirely. At the other end of the scale, "job
rotation to develop the generalist rather than
the specialist" came in last as the feature least
employed by the Japanese companies again in both
Hong Kong and Singapore, 55 per cent and 74 per
cent of them respectively stating that it is not
employed at all. Taken together, the survey
findings present a rather confusing picture
regarding the employment of features of Japanese-
style management in East Asia. Perhaps we should
remind ourselves that those features included in
the questionnaire are typically adopted by large
businesses but not necessarily by smaller
businesses in Japan. Although the companies
selected in this survey are all subsidiaries of
large well-known companies in Japan, their

Figure 6-1: Employment of Japanese-style Management Features

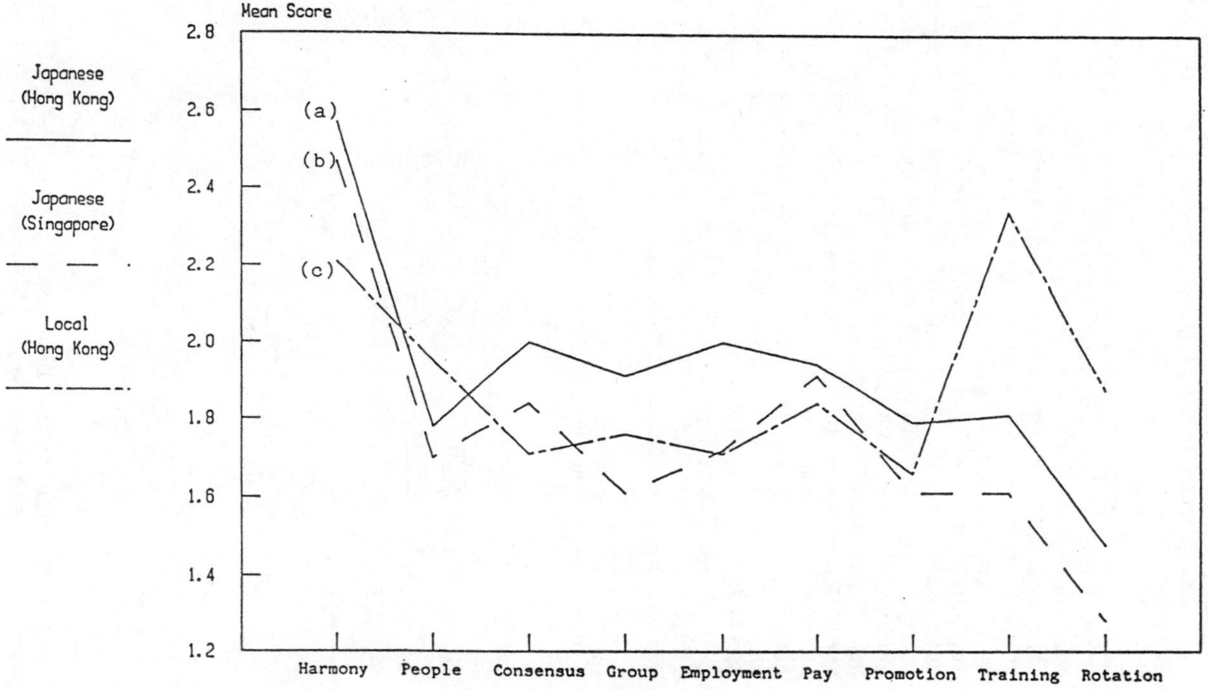

Japan, their operation in Hong Kong or Singapore is rather small, employing only around 150 on the average.

By sharp contrast, "on-the-job training" came in first as the feature employed the most by local companies in Hong Kong, 42 per cent of whom stating that it is employed entirely. On the other hand, "seniority-based promotion system" turned out to be the feature employed the least by them, over 40 per cent stating that it is not employed at all. Compared with the Japanese companies operating in Hong Kong or Singapore, the local companies are placing much greater emphasis on their employees' training and development. This could be largely due to their much larger size of operation. The average number of employees among the selected local companies is nearly 2,000. Considering that only about 2 per cent of the total of some 300,000 business establishments in Hong Kong employ 100 or more workers, all these local companies included in our survey should be regarded as the giants by Hong Kong standards.

Figure 6-2: Cross-cultural Differences and
Similarities in Management

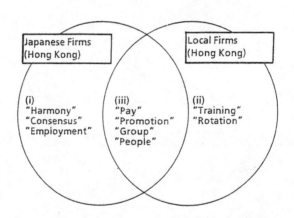

The distance between lines (a) and (c) in Figure 6-1 shows a difference in the extent of employing a given feature of management between the Japanese and local companies in Hong Kong, i.e. cross-cultural differences. Figure 6-2

similarities, by categorizing the nine features examined into three types:

i) Those employed much more by the Japanese companies.

ii) Those employed much more by the local companies.

iii) Those employed (or unemployed) more or less to the same extent by the two groups of companies.

On the one hand, it would appear that the Japanese companies, as a group, are employing features such as group harmony, decision-making by consensus and the lifetime employment system to a much greater extent than their Hong Kong counterparts. On the other hand, they seem to be only too cautious about the introduction of on-the-job training and job rotation into their Hong Kong operations, employing these two particular features even to a lesser extent than their local counterparts. Figure 6-2 also shows that the Japanese companies have adapted to the local conditions in regard to the employment (or non-employment) of management features such as the seniority-based pay system, seniority-based promotion system and group responsibility system.

MANAGEMENT ACROSS COUNTRIES AND CULTURES

Though useful in getting a rough picture, the comparative analysis above was simply based on the averages of aggregate scores obtained by each group of companies. However, there were varying degrees of dispersion among the individual responses even within the same group. As explained in Figure 6-3, a high mean score and a low standard deviation indicates that the feature is employed to a large extent and with strong group consensus among the sample companies. By classifying the features by mean scores and standard deviations, we should be able to carry out a more meaningful comparative analysis.

Figure 6-3: Four Categories of Management Features

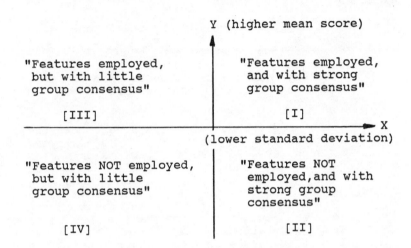

Figure 6-4 has been prepared to compare the two groups of Japanese companies operating in Hong Kong and Singapore according to this classification. It shows:

* "Harmony" and "pay" features are employed to a large to fair extent; and there is strong group consensus as to their employment in Hong Kong and also in Singapore. The two features thus fall in Quadrant I. Furthermore, in both countries, there is strong consensus against the employment of "training", "promotion", "people", and "rotation"; all four features fall in Quadrant II.
* Despite these cross-national similarities, there are some differences as well. "Consensus", "employment", and "group" features are employed to a fair extent in Hong Kong, though not necessarily with strong consensus (Quadrant III). The same features fall in Quadrant IV in the case of Japanese companies in Singapore.
* While the features at the highest and lowest points on Y-axis (i.e. "harmony" and "rotation") as well as those at the left-most and right-most points on X-axis (i.e. "consensus" and "pay") are the same, the size of a diamond formed by connecting these four

points is different. The taller and wider "Singapore diamond" suggests that the Japanese companies in Singapore, as a group, are not only more selective but also more divergent in their individual views on the employment of Japanese-style management features.

* The "Singapore diamond" is positioned to the south-east (i.e. toward a lower mean-score and standard deviation) of the "Hong Kong diamond", indicating that the group of Japanese companies in Singapore has relatively stronger consensus against the wholesale transfer of Japanese management.

Whereas the cross-national comparison of companies above has shown more similarities than differences in the extent and consensus for or against employing what are considered as the unique features of Japanese-style management, cross-cultural comparison of companies, which operate in the same territory but have different cultural origins, seems to point to more differences than similarities. Figure 6-5, prepared now to compare the Japanese and local companies operating in Hong Kong, shows:

* There is only one feature ("people") that is employed to a fair extent and with strong group consensus among the local companies in Hong Kong (Quadrant I). But this very feature is one of those not much employed, and with strong group consensus, in the case of Japanese companies in Hong Kong (Quadrant II).
* Six out of nine features included in the study (i.e. rotation, pay, group, employment, consensus, and promotion) are little employed by the local companies, though there is no particularly strong group consensus against their employment (Quadrant IV). This is in contrast to the fact that there is not a single feature falling in this category in the case of Japanese companies in Hong Kong.
* The group of Japanese companies in Hong Kong has strong consensus against the employment of "training", "promotion", "people", and "rotation". These four features fall in Quadrant II, but there is not even one feature belonging to this category in the case of local companies.

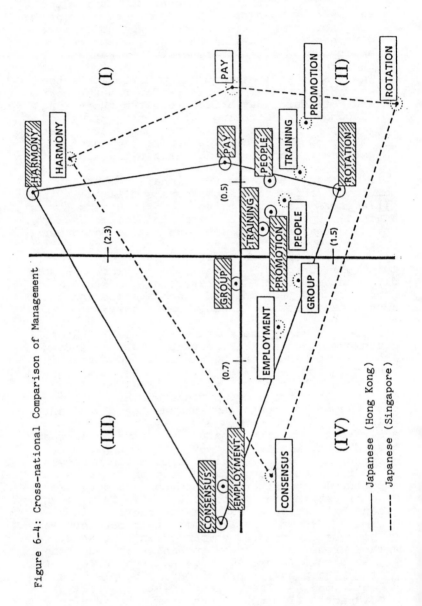

Figure 6-4: Cross-national Comparison of Management

—— Japanese (Hong Kong)
----- Japanese (Singapore)

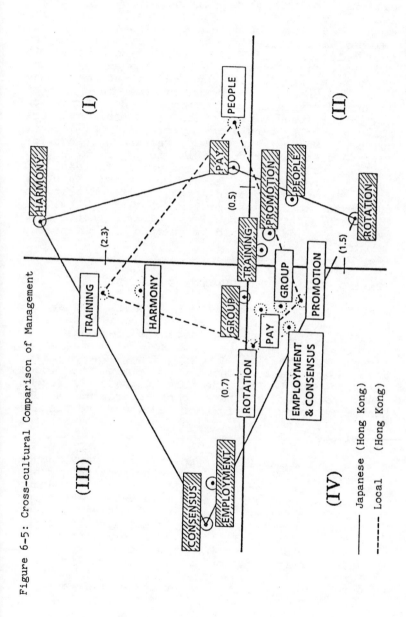

Figure 6-5: Cross-cultural Comparison of Management

—— Japanese (Hong Kong)
------ Local (Hong Kong)

143

Figure 6-5 also shows that "emphasis on group harmony" and "total concern for people" are employed to a large to fair degree by Hong Kong's local companies. These two features are considered attributable to Japan's cultural values, and represent the corporate ideologies typically adopted by Japanese companies in Japan. As a matter of fact, the extent of the employment of "total concern for people" by the local companies is somewhat greater than that of Japanese companies operating in Hong Kong. On the other hand, two other features, which are also generally considered attributable to Japan's cultural values (i.e. group, rather than individual, duties and responsibilities, and collective decision-making by consensus) are little employed in practice by the local companies. In other words, despite a notable degree of similarity in corporate ideologies (i.e. "what they believe in"), the actual practices of management (i.e. "what they do") could be quite different across cultures.

STAYING CLEAR OF THE WHOLESALE EXPORT

Operating in the environment which is similar but not exactly the same as their own in the home country, few Japanese companies seem to have attempted to export wholesale Japanese-style management practices to Hong Kong. The majority have, in fact, chosen to adopt the local practices to a considerable degree. A recent study of four Japanese banks operating in Hong Kong has provided further evidence to confirm this [8]. The study findings can be summarized as follows:

* The organizational power is very much concentrated in the hands of top executives, who are coincidentally all Japanese expatriates; and little information about the organization is given out to people lower down. Needless to say, the concentration of power and monopolization of information at the top would not allow the local employees' active participation in management process. For one, the absence of a Quality Control Circle - a widely used practice in Japan - in

three out of four sample companies studied suggests a lack of participation in decision-making on the part of local employees.

* The work in Japanese companies in Japan is more often than not assigned on a group basis with only vague stipulation of individual duties and responsibilities. In other words, there is no distinct job demarcation, and employees are expected to perform their duties regardless of what may be prescribed in the work manual. Of the four banks surveyed, only one employs this particular feature of Japanese-style management, and one bank does not employ it at all. The remaining two banks take the middle-of-the-road approach by assigning work on a group basis and then defining an individual's duties and responsibilities to demarcate jobs within the group.

* All four Japanese subsidiaries do not lay off their employees unless they have committed serious wrongs. However, the life-time employment system, if interpreted strictly as job-security until retirement age, is applied only to Japanese expatriates. For local employees, the companies simply try to retain them by providing better-than-average fringe benefits by the local standards. The benefits include medical allowance, provident fund, housing loan subsidy for senior staff, twice-a-year bonus, gifts and petty cash loan.

* The seniority-based pay system is not employed by any Japanese bank studied. Instead, the annual salary increment is largely based on the result of an appraisal report, often incorporating self-appraisal by employees. The appraisal is also used to help determine the amount of bonus, promotion, and the need for further training. As for the promotion system, importance is placed on both seniority and ability. While bank clerks are usually promoted one grade each year, advancement to officer grade and above depends more on ability. Though the first priority in filling a vacancy at the higher level position is to promote from within, employing a well-qualified outsider is not unusual.

* On-the-job training is largely limited to those at the officer grade and above. Those selected for training are also sent to the parent company in Japan, either on a regular or irregular basis. Job rotation within and/or across departments is provided only to the long-serving employees, who are in most cases at the officer grade and above. For other employees, this practice is only employed to a very limited extent.

Table 6-3: Japanese Management Practices in Singapore (N=6)

Participation in planning	Mainly Japanese managers	(6)
	Mainly local managers	(0)
Individual job description	Available	(2)
	Not available	(4)
Employment system	Permanent employment	(5)
	Hire and fire	(1)
Promotion system	Seniority-based	(1)
	Merit-based	(5)
Pay system	Seniority-based	(4)
	Merit-based	(2)
Training (Executives)	Formal training	(3)
	On-the-job training	(3)
Training (Blue collar workers)	Formal training	(0)
	On-the-job training	(6)
Job rotation	Limited rotation	(1)
	No rotation	(5)

[Putti, J.M. and T. Chong, 1985, p.112]

Similarly, an in-depth study of six Japanese manufacturing subsidiaries in Singapore has also revealed that the management practices of Japanese companies operating in the country are not necessarily the same as those of their parent organizations in Japan [9]. Table 6-3 presents the extract of findings from the study. It

146

appears that the people involved in the planning
process are mainly Japanese expatriates sent in
from Japan. Though all the Japanese companies
surveyed encourage their local employees to
forward suggestions to their immediate superiors,
only one company admitted to using the "ringi"
system of decision-making. Another company uses
it only among the Japanese. Without the
delegation of authority in decision-making to the
lower levels, the organizational power is almost
exclusively in the hands of Japanese expatriate
managers. A job description for every job is not
a common feature in the Japanese companies
surveyed in Singapore. Even when it exists, it
is only used as guidelines.

Life-time employment system is apparently
present, if one interprets this to mean job
security or no dismissal for non-performance; the
Japanese companies studied all seem to be only
willing to adopt this system. However, they face
the problem of high employee turnover due to a
low degree of loyalty to the company on the part
of Singaporean workers. This is despite strong
support for group activities through financial
subsidies to recreational facilities and programs
as well as the presence of Japanese managers at
the company-organized social functions, all aimed
at generating the feeling of oneness with the
company. Perhaps, as a consequence, generous
fringe benefits are generally absent from the
Japanese companies in Singapore.

Only one out of six companies studied
practices the seniority-based promotion system
to the letter. Others have either reduced the
weighting of seniority or almost totally
discarded the system, relying more on ability and
performance record. Still, seniority is taken
into consideration in determining salaries and
bonuses in four companies. Job rotation is not
widely practiced; training is largely on-the-job,
particularly for blue-collar workers. In three
companies, senior Japanese executives conduct
formal management development courses for their
local management employees. In addition, the same
number of companies send their supervisory staff
for training in Japan; and engineers in all
companies are sent to Japan for technical
training whenever the need arises.

Singapore is a cosmopolitan and hetero-
geneous society. With neither the homogeneity
nor insularity of Japanese society, Singapore's

economic development has all along been based on individualistic competition. Though a large part of the population's forefathers imbibed much of Confucius' teachings, the education system that is largely Western in design has produced "go-getters" bent on achieving individual and instant success [10]. In the face of such values of individualism, the introduction of the Japanese corporate ideology of group-orientation, in its pure form, could be difficult. The same would also apply to Hong Kong. Operating in the environment which is different from their own, Japanese companies operating in Hong Kong or Singapore appear to have transplanted to date the features of their home-grown management only to a minuscule degree.

MOVING TO BECOME TRUE MULTINATIONALS

One may assume that the cultural similarity in East Asia will make the local employees think and behave very much like the Japanese. The nation's cultural values affect the values of organizational culture as often expressed in the corporate ideologies. Our study in Hong Kong, for one, has found that the local companies hold corporate ideologies similar to those typically held by Japanese companies in Japan. In this case, then, it should not be a very difficult task to transfer the features of Japanese-style management to the region. However, the study has also indicated that what the people believe in is not always translated into what they actually do. Or perhaps, it would be more accurate to say that even if the people think in a similar way, they may behave rather differently. In fact, after a few years at the overseas posts in Hong Kong or Singapore, many Japanese managers seem to have come to realize the difficulty in transplanting their home country practices of management onto Asian soil. Today, Japanese companies operating in the region are managed without any strong group consensus as to what the best practices might be. For example, the seniority-based pay system has been adopted to a fair extent with strong consensus. On the other hand, the introduction of collective decision-making by consensus has been attempted, but there is little consensus either for or against its employment.

148

The traditional Japanese-style management is unquestionably underpinned by a deep core of Japan's cultural values. Some of its features are indeed largely attributable to cultural values, while others may be related more to economic incentives. It could be said that Japanese-style management is not complete unless the features related to both cultural values and economic incentives are actually employed in practice. Obviously, the employment of certain culture-related features have encountered some difficulty, even on Asian soil. The transfer of management features more directly related to economic incentives might be considered relatively easy. These features include: the life-time employment system, seniority-based pay and promotion system, on-the-job training, and job rotation. However, most of these features are little employed in practice by Japanese companies operating in East Asia.

The difficulty being experienced at present by Japanese companies in transplanting the features of Japanese-style management could be explained, in large part, by their relatively short history and small-scale operations abroad. Perhaps, as the companies get better established on foreign soils and expand their operations, a wider employment of some of these features could become feasible, leading to the practice of more complete Japanese-style management. In the meantime, many a Japanese company, with an ambition to become a truly internationalized multinational, seems to be going through the active learning process in order to determine exactly which features are to be exported and how they should be modified for a successful transplantation outside Japan.

NOTES

1. Fortune International, "Japan is the Rich Neighbour Everyone Loves to Hate", (Mar. 30, 1987), p.43
2. Kazer, W., "Japanese Firms Investing in Asia to Offset Rising Yen", Business News (South China Morning Post, Jul. 4, 1987), p.3

3. Matsuura, K., "Japan's Overseas Investment and Hong Kong", mimeograph, Hong Kong: Japan
Information and Cultural Office, (Mar. 1987)

4. Roscoe, B., "Japanese Business Moves
Offshore - Slowly", Far Eastern Economic Review,
(Apr. 30, 1987), p.74

5. Thurley, K., M. Nangaku and K. Urugami,
"Employment Relations of Japanese Companies in
the UK: A Report on an Exploratory Study",
mimeograph, London: Association for Japanese
Studies, (1978)

6. Trevor, M., "Does Japanese Management
Work in Britain?", Journal of General Management,
(summer 1983), pp.28-43

7. The Oriental Economist, "Japanese-style
Management on Trial in America", (Sept. 1983),
pp.8-13

8. Tang, K.M., "Human Resource Management at
Japanese Banks in Hong Kong", project report,
Department of Business & Management, City Poly-
technic of Hong Kong, (May 1987)

9. Putti, J.M. and T. Chong, "American and
Japanese Management Practices in Their Singapore
Subsidiaries", Asian Pacific Journal of
Management, (Jan. 1985), pp.106-114

10. ibid.

Chapter Seven

CHINESE WORKERS UNDER JAPANESE MANAGEMENT - ARE THEY HAPPY?

Japanese companies are said to retain a happy work-force highly motivated and satisfied to contribute to the success of the company. Their employees show a deep, long-term commitment to the company - a commitment which is reciprocated by the company as well reflected in the ideologies and practices of its management. It must be be noted, however, that much of Japanese-style management is supported by the nation's cultural foundations; the same supports are generally not available in other cultures, or only to a lesser degree. Moreover, some of the features may be rejected as incompatible with the institutions or customs of the host country. As a result, many Japanese companies which have ventured out to set up operations overseas appear to be having difficulties in managing their local workers in different cultures. For one, the level of motivation and job satisfaction among local workers employed by Japanese companies is not always as high as hoped for by the management. In this chapter, we will first examine the theories of movitation, developed and well-tested in the US, and their applicability in other cultures. This will be followed by the presentation of findings from the Worker Opinion Survey that was conducted at the overseas branches of a large Japanese company operating in two of Asia's newly-industrialized countries whose population is predominantly Chinese - Hong Kong and Singapore. It is hoped that the analysis of the survey findings can help us find out how happy the non-Japanese workers are under Japanese management and identify the causes of problems being experienced by Japanese companies in East Asia.

CULTURE AND MOTIVATION

The cultual orientation of a society reflects values with attitudinal and behavioral implications. For example, assumptions about basic human nature range from "good" to "evil". McGregor's Theory X and Theory Y describe these two sets of assumptions about the nature of human beings and what they want from their work environment as follows [1]:

Theory X - People are basically evil, lazy, irresponsible, and dumb. The average person has an inherent dislike of work and will avoid it, if possible.

Theory Y - People are basically good, industrious, responsible, and smart. For the average person, the expenditure of physical and mental effort in work is as natural as play.

Based on the said assumption, Theory X leaders believe that people must be coerced, controlled, directed or threatened with punishments in order to motivate them to work. By contrast, Theory Y leaders believe that most people will exercise self-direction and self-control, and must be given freedom, autonomy, and responsibility. Such summary statements reflect polar opposites which, admittedly, are unrealistic. Human beings are neither completely evil nor completely good. However, the basic assumption the leader makes can have a significant impact on organization and management. Though there is strong evidence that a managerial system paralleling Theory Y makes significantly better use of human resources and enhances both efficiency and effectiveness of organizational endeavour, managers in a wide range of cultures vary in their reasons for making the Theory X or Theory Y assumption [2]. In some countries such as the US, managers want to be seen as decision-makers and professionally competent leaders, whereas in other countries such as Japan, managers want to regard themselves more as the facilitators of decision-making and social leaders. In short, the appropriate leadership of management is culturally contingent.

Beyond culturally appropriate leadership-style, what will motivate people to work in a given culture and situation? The theories of motivation address this question. Motivation is not a simple concept. The psychologists maintain that "one of the most difficult tasks is to describe the urge behind behavior; the motivation of any organism, even the simplest one, is at present only partly understood" [3]. Skinner, for example, has explained that an individual is a black box wherein feeling and thought processes are unknown and unknowable; behavior occurs and is directed, amplified, and sustained via the conditioning effects of reinforcements [4].

In spite of the difficulty involved, researchers have attempted to explain why people think and behave in the ways they do and what managers can do to encourage certain types of behavior while discouraging others. Many have examined internal states and processes of individuals - needs, values, and expectations. The key idea is that it is important to understand what people feel and how they think in order to predict how they will behave in a given situation. This view of motivation has been approached via two dimensions - what motivates people (content) and how behavior is produced (process). The content approach focuses on the specific variables that influence behavior, such as internal needs and values or external conditions. The process approach also attempts to identify major variables that explain behavior, but the main focus is on the dynamics of how the variables are interrelated [5]. Let us now look at three major motivation theories and see whether they are universal or culture-bound.

Maslow's Need Hierarchy Theory

The Need Hierarchy Theory was developed by Maslow, an American psychologist, who suggested that human beings have five relatively separate and distinct needs: physiological, security, social, esteem, and self-actualization needs (see Table 7-1). According to Maslow, the average person is satisfied 85 per cent in physiological needs, 70 per cent in security needs, 50 per cent in social needs, 40 per cent in esteem needs, and 10 per cent in self-actualization needs [6].

The theory suggests that the human needs form a hierarchy, upward from physiological to self-actualization needs, with the higher needs becoming activated, and thus motivating behavior, after lower needs have been satisfied. While human needs could be separated and arranged in a hierarchy of importance for analysis and understanding, they are probably all active in actual behavioral patterns. Moreover, the needs, particularly those at the lower level, are never completely satisfied. They recur periodically, and if their satisfaction is deprived for any period of time, they become potent as motivators for action. It is conceivable that the relative importance of the needs changes during an individual's life; the lower needs are dominant early in life with the higher needs becoming more important as a person matures. It may also vary depending on the level of education that an individual has received; the more educated person tends to rank self-actualiztion as more important and security as less important than do the less educated one [7].

Table 7-1: Hierarchy of Human Needs

Self-actualization needs	Achieving the potential within oneself, maximum self-development creativity, and self-expression.
Esteem needs	Self-respect, respect of others, and ego or status.
Social needs	Association with others, belonging to groups, and giving and receiving friendship and affection.
Security needs	Protection against danger, threat, and deprivation.
Physiological needs	Hunger, thirst, sleep, sex, and evacuation.

It should be noted that Maslow's theory is based on the Americans, and it may not hold for workers outside the US. In fact, several studies which tested Maslow's hierarchy demonstrated similar but not identical rank ordering of the needs across cultures. An individual's frame of reference will determine the order of importance of his needs, and his frame of reference is in part determined by his culture; therefore, it can be said that an individual's needs are partially bound by culure [8].

In examining the applicability of American theories of motivation abroad, Hofstede noted that in countries high on uncertainty avoidance, such as Japan, workers consider security as more important than self-actualization; workers in collective countries, such as Japan, tend to stress social needs over more individualistic esteem and self-actualization needs [9]. Another large-scale study of a US multinational company operating in 46 countries also pointed out some significant differences across cultures. English-speaking countries are higher on individual achievement and lower on the desire for security; French-speaking countries, while similar to English-speaking countries, give greater importance to security and somewhat less to challenging work; Latin countries find individual achievement somewhat less important, especially Southern Europeans who place the highest emphasis on job security; Japan is low on advancement, with strong emphasis on good working conditions and a friendly working environment [10].

Human needs identified by Maslow might include fundamental or universal aspects, but their relative importance and the ways they are expressed in actual behavior could vary from one culture to another. While the Need Hierarchy Theory may be considered as a good first approximation in understanding human motivation and in predicting behavior, there are significant individual differences that must be recognized in any given culture and situation.

Herzberg's Two Factor Theory

Herzberg suggested that all human needs could be classified into two separate and essentially unrelated types - physical needs and psychological needs [11]. He argued that when physical needs were satisfied, they induced a feeling of relief from discomfort. But relief from discomfort is no way related to pleasure or satisfaction and, therefore, physical needs are merely hygiene factors or dissatisfiers. If they exist in a work environment in high quantity, they will yield no dissatisfaction. On the other hand, when psychological needs are satisfied, they induce a feeling of pleasure or satisfaction and, therefore, psychological needs are motivating factors or satisfiers. Their existence will yield a feeling of satisfaction.

In essence, Herzberg's Two Factor Theory suggests that hygiene factors only have the power to demotivate, while motivating factors have the power to motivate or energize behavior. Hygiene factors are associated with the environment surrounding a job, and closely correspond to Maslow's physiological, security, and social needs. They include factors associated with job dissatisfaction such as pay, company policy and administration, working conditions, job security, relations with co-workers, and quality of supervision. Motivating factors are associated with the job content, and correspond to Maslow's higher order needs. They include factors associated with job satisfaction such as challenging work, responsibility, recognition, advancement, and achievement. The relationship of the hygiene and motivating factors to Maslow's Need Hierarchy is shown in Table 7-2.

In some countries, the factors which are regarded merely as hygiene factors by Herzberg have been cited as motivating factors. For example, in New Zealand, the quality of supervision and relations with co-workers appear to contribute significantly to job satisfaction and not merely to reducing dissatisfaction [12]. To a large degree, the same would apply in Japan. As the specific factors and their relative importance are particular to each culture, the universality of Herzberg's Two Factor Theory cannot be assumed.

Table 7-2: Relationship between Maslow's and
Herzberg's Theories of Motivation

Maslow's Need Hierarchy	Herzberg's		
	Classification of Needs	Hygiene Factors	Motivating Factors
Self-Actualization	Psychological		Challenging Work Achievement Responsibility
Esteem			Recognition Advancement
Social		Co-workers Supervision	
Security	Physical	Policy/Admin. Job Security	
Physiological		Pay, Working Conditions	

Vroom's Expectancy Theory

Criticizing Maslow's and Herzberg's theories of
motivation as being too dependent on the content
and context of the work roles of people, Vroom
offered an alternative approach to the understanding of motivation [13].   The essential
element of his Expectancy Theory is that people
will be motivated to do things to the extent of
expectation that a certain action on their part
will help them achieve desired outcomes.   In
other words, the strength of an individual's
motivation toward an action will be determined by
the anticipated values of the outcomes of his
action multiplied by the probability that the
action will yield the desired outcomes in some
form of rewards.   Simply put, Vroom's theory
states that:

Force = Valence x Expectacy

where "Force" is the strength of an
individual's motivation; "Valence" is
the attractiveness of outcomes; and
"Expectancy" is the likelihood that an
action will lead to desired outcomes.

As expressed in the model above, the force exerted to do something will depend on both valence and expectacy. If an individual were indifferent or even negative about a certain outcome (i.e. the valence is zero or negative), he would have no motivation. Likewise, a person would not be motivated to act, unless the probability of achieving the outcome were positive (i.e. the expectancy is greater than zero). The validity of the Expectancy Theory depends on the extent to which employees believe that they have control over the outcomes of their efforts as well as on the manager's ability to identify the type of rewards desired by employees, both of which surely vary across cultures [14].

While the theory is no doulbt helpful in visualizing the complexity involved in understanding and predicting an individual's behavior, it is culturally dependent. For example, the Americans generally see themselves as dominant over their environment, and believe they can control it. The Japanese, on the other hand, want to live in harmony with the surrounding environment; people in some other cultures see themselves subjugated by nature, and tend to accept the inevitable forces of nature. In these cultures outside the US, employees believe that they have only partial or no control over their working environment and the outcomes of their own actions. The rewards people want from work also vary considerably across cultures. In the individual-oriented societies such as the US, people value individualistic rewards such as recognition and advancement. By contrast, in the group-oriented societies such as Japan, people tend to value the group's welfare over the individualistic rewards. The universality of Vroom's Expectancy Theory cannot be assumed. However, when modified for the extent to which people believe that they control their work environment and for the type of rewards desired, this theory developed in the US appears to hold even in countries as culturally dissmilar to the US as Japan [15].

In summary, Maslow's Need Hierarchy Theory identifies and ranks human needs according to their importance; Herzberg's Two Factor Theory classifies them into hygiene factors and motivating factors; Vroom's Expectancy Theory suggests that the strength of an individual's motivation depends on the expectation that his action will produce desired outcomes. Put together, the theories attempt to explain what basic needs people have, which of these needs really motivate people, and how action is produced in order to satisfy the needs. And, as shown in Figure 7-1, there exists a complex interaction of needs, motivation, action, and satisfaction.

Figure 7-1: Needs, Motivation, Action, and Satisfaction

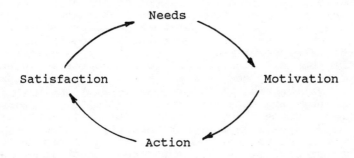

Motivation refers to the drive for action to satisfy a need; satisfaction refers to the contentment experienced when the need is fulfilled. In other words, motivation implies a drive toward outcomes, while satisfaction involves outcomes already experienced. Motivation and satisfaction are to be considered as two inseparable ingredients of employees' happiness at work; both are needed to retain a happy work-force. A person may have high motivation for the job but low job satisfaction, or the reverse may be true. There is understandably the high probability that a highly motivated individual with low job satisfaction will look for another job in a different organization. In reference to Herzberg's Two Factor Theory, one could argue that a highly motivated person will leave the organization because of a lack of motivating factors that will yield a real feeling of satisfaction. Alternatively, in reference to Vroom's Expectancy Theory, this could be explained by a person's weakened motivation due to a loss of the attractiveness of rewards and/or a lowered expectation that his action will actually produce desired outcomes.

APPLICABILITY OF AMERICAN THEORIES

Like most other theories of management, the three theories of motivation that we have just examined were developed in the US by the Americans and for the Americans. Therefore, they necessarily reflect the cultural values of the Americans, and they may not offer universal explanations of motivation. In fact, there is evidence that the use of the American work motivation concepts and techniques is even detrimental to organizational effectiveness in other cultures [16]. Still, in the absence of well-developed theories elsewhere, the basic concepts of these theories could well provide a good start in understanding human motivation and behavior even outside the US. Let us now evaluate their applicability in the East Asian context by examining the findings from three surveys carried out recently in Hong Kong.

A survey of 124 middle-level managers from 25 organizations, which was conducted with an aim to find out the perceived importance of Job Satisfaction (JS) attributes, has revealed the JS attributes that have direct effects on the individuals such as financial rewards, opportunities for promotion, and challenging work are regarded as most important; the attributes that are interpersonal in nature such as relationships with co-workers and supervisors are regarded as somewhat less important; job security and working conditions at the company are regarded as least important [17]. A survey of college students in Hong Kong majoring in business management (i.e. the future managers) confirmed the above findings [18]. Likewise, a survey of 145 middle-level managers, all working in the same organization, also produced similar findings, though the respondents here placed a relatively greater importance on job security and working conditions and somewhat less importance on opportunities for promotion than those in the other surveys did [19]. A summary of findings from the three separate surveys above is presented in in Table 7-3.

The findings generally support Herzberg's Motivation Theory in that challenging work (job itself) and opportunities for advancement (promotion) are regarded as the prime motivators; importance placed on them is clearly reflective of a desire for self-actualization and esteem. Hofstede's study on international differences in work-related values has also found that people in Hong Kong, as well as in Singapore, are highly motivated by personal success [20]. However, the surveys in Hong Kong have indicated that financial rewards (pay), which are merely regarded as a hygiene factor by Herzberg, are in fact one of the most important motivators.

Table 7-3: Ranking Order of Perceived Importance of Job Satisfaction Attributes in Hong Kong

Ranking	Study I	Study II	Study III
1	Pay	Job Itself *	Pay
2	Promotion *	Promotion *	Job Itself *
3	Job Itself *	Pay	Company
4	Supervisors	Co-workers	Promotion *
5	Co-workers	Supervisors	Co-workers
6	Company	Company	Supervisors

* Note: These are considered as the motivating factors by Herzberg.

The importance of money as a motivator has been consistently down-graded by most researchers in the US; they have pointed out the value of challenging work, participation in decision-making, and other non-monetary factors as stimulants to employee motivation [21]. However, people in Hong Kong appear to have a much greater expectation that any personal success must be matched with monetary rewards. This pattern is actually consistent with the post-

industrialization hypothesis which suggests that
in developing or newly-industrialized countries
such as Hong Kong and Singapore, materialistic
values are highly endorsed, whereas in highly-
developed countries such as the US, values
emphasizing non-monetary factors are more
dominant [22].

Although individualistic job enrichment
programs designed and used in the US could be
useful in Hong Kong or Singapore, their
effectiveness may have to be discounted somewhat
because people in the newly-industrialized
countries regard money as relatively more
important and challenging work as less important
than their American counterparts do. Such an
individualistic pattern of preferences may make
it hard to induce a feeling of commitment
and loyalty to the company among employees.
Challenging work is not simply good enough;
employees will leave for a job that pays more
[23].

The findings from the surveys of practicing
and future managers in Hong Kong, together with
our earlier review of the literature, can be
summed up as follows. (a) The order of the
perceived importance of an individual's needs
varies across cultures. Workers in Japan tend to
stress social and security needs over
individualistic self-actualization and esteem
needs, which are generally stressed by workers in
the US. Workers in Hong Kong, like their
counterparts in the US, tend to stress personal
success over congenial interpersonal relationships and job security. However, they regard
financial rewards as more important and
challenging work as relatively less important
than American workers do. (b) In every culture,
certain factors act as motivating factors, while
others act as hygiene factors. In Japan, the
quality of supervision, relations with
co-workers, and the company as a whole contribute
significantly to job satisfaction, and they are
generally regarded as motivating factors. By
contrast, these same factors are merely regarded
as hygiene factors in Hong Kong. (c) The rewards
people want and the extent of belief that they
have control over the surrounding environment may
vary across cultures, sometimes to a marked
degree. In Japan, people try to live in harmony
with the environment, rather than controlling
it. The Japanese value the group's welfare over

individualistic rewards such as personal recognition and advancement. People in Hong Kong may also hold more or less the same view about the environment, but they tend to value more individualistic rewards, especially monetary rewards.

There are indeed significant differences across cultures, even within the East Asian context, in the ranking order of importance and classification of human needs as well as in the primary basis of human behavior. This may pose some problems to Japanese companies operating in East Asia.

WORKER OPINION SURVEY

A popular myth states that hygiene factors are enough to satisfy workers, while motivating factors should be considered when dealing with managers. Contrary to the myth, a study of 178 non-managerial staff in Hong Hong has shown that job-related factors such as challenging work, opportunities for promotion and financial rewards are also perceived by workers as most important while the factors associated with interpersonal relationships are least important [24]. In other words, non-managerial workers are not any different from managers in ranking the order of importance of their needs. It does seem that the hygiene-motivator concept applies to people in all walks of life and at all levels [25]. As Kast and Rosenzweig put it, the dichotomy between managers and workers is unfortunate because it perpetuates a chasm between subsystems of organizations that really should be integrated for effectiveness and efficient performance; all are managers, all are workers; there is no way to draw a meaningful line of demarcation [26].

Against this background, the Worker Opinion Survey was conducted to investigate how well the needs of workers were fulfilled by measuring the level of satisfaction with work-related factors among the local employees working at the overseas branches of a major Japanese department-store operating in Hong Kong and Singapore. The parent company was established in Tokyo more than 60 years ago, and today it employs over 6,000 workers. There were three reasons for selecting the department-store as the object of our study.

Firstly, the service-sector investment which aims at providing business services (e.g. wholesale, retail, finance, banking), is the latest type of Japan's direct investment overseas that only began to rush into Asia's newly-industrialized countries such as Hong Kong and Singapore in the mid-1980s. As a result, very little has been studied to date about this sector. Secondly, our survey, which examined the practices of Japanese management in Hong Kong and Singapore (see Chapter six), indicated that the extent of the actual employment of the features of Japanese-style management was consistently greater in the service-sector than in the manufacturing, engineering, construction and other sectors. It would, therefore, be interesting to find out the level of job satisfaction among the local employees working in this particular sector. Thirdly, of all the Japanese businesses in Hong Kong or Singapore, perhaps the publicly most visible ones are department-stores. Since the first Japanese department-store in Hong Kong was established back in 1960, two arrived in the 1970s followed by six more in the 1980s. There are nearly 47,000 retail establishments in Hong Kong, employing over 160,000 people. In the field of some 100 department-stores of various sizes and origins, the nine Japanese stores as a group will unquestionably continue to play the role of the trend-setter and market-leader. A similarly important role is being played by five Japanese department-stores which have successively opened the door for business in Singapore over the past sixteen years. Competing fiercely among themselves and against other local stores in the small but lucrative retail market, the management of the department-store is naturally very interested in finding out how satisfied their own local employees are.

The Hong Kong branch of the Japanese department-store selected for our study was opened in 1973, and has nearly 200 local Chinese employees on its payroll. It is run by a team of four Japanese and three Chinese managers. In a pre-survey interview, the General Manager stated that the company's slogan - "Everyone is good and equal" - could best represent the corporate management philosophy. He said, "We actually translate this philosophy, long adopted at the parent company in Tokyo, into practice at this branch, too. As a matter of fact, all the managers here, including myself, have got to where we are now from the very bottom - cleaning and dusting, selling, taking inventory, and so on." However, he lamented that he still did not quite understand the mind of the local people even after ten years as the head of the Hong Kong branch. And the only problem, that he has not found an answer for yet, is a lack of employees' loyalty to the company.

The Singapore branch, which today has some 600 mostly ethnic Chinese employees on its payroll, was established in 1971. This first Japanese department-store in Singapore is run by six Japanese managers and the same number of Singaporian managers. The local managers are all ethnic Chinese, with the average of nearly twelve years of service at the company. The General Manager, who was sent in from Tokyo two years ago, also singled out a lack of employees' loyalty to the company as the only serious management problem that he has encountered so far. He also admitted a great difficulty in instituting the effective in-house training and development programs in the light of an extremely high labor turnover among the sales personnel.

Sixty-two and 65 sales personnel, randomly selected in Hong Kong and Singapore, respectively, participated in our survey. To measure their job satisfaction, it was decided to adopt an instrument developed in the UK for its tested reliability and validity [27]. The multidimensional questionnaire, written in both English and Chinese for self-completion, consisted of 48 question-items with 8 items each under 6 main categories (See table 7-4). Though it was initially felt that it might be necessary to localize the survey instrument, discussions with the personnel manager and a subsequent pilot study gave a sufficient indication as to the validity of the instrument for use both in Hong Kong and Singapore. The question-items were presented in blocks covering each category. A response to a given question could be "Yes", "?" (for uncertainty, if one cannot decide), or "No". A traditional scoring frame was used: 2, 1, or 0, with 2 indicating the highest degree of satisfaction. Half the items in each category, those indicated by "*", were reverse scored.

Table 7-4: Worker Opinion Survey - Categories of
            Question-Items

Category	Question-Item
Job Itself	"It's the same day after day"* "The wrong sort of job for me"* "Worthwhile" "Routine"* "Time passes quickly" "Satisfying" "Better than other jobs I have had" "Endless"*
Present Pay	"Underpaid for what I do"* "Adequate for my needs" "Far too low"* "Quite highly paid" "Fairly satisfactory" "Poor"* "Well paid" "Less than I deserve"*
Opportunities for Promotion	"The system for promotion is fair" "Prospect very limited"* "Easy to get on" "Too much favoritism"* "Good opportunities" "Experience increases my prospects" "Dead-end job"* "Good jobs are taken before I know"
Immediate Superior	"Lets me know where I stand" "Does a good job" "Interferes too much"* "Always too busy to see me"* "Stands up for me" "Quick tempered"* "Can discuss problems with him" "Hard to please"
People I Work With	"Easy to make enemies" "Hard working" "Some think they run the place"* "Know their job" "Work well as a group" "Stupid"* "Unpleasant"* "Do their share of work"
Company as a Whole	"Looks after its employees" "A poor company to work for"* "They treat me like a number"* "Has a good reputation" "Too much class distinction"* "Makes me feel I belong" "Need fresh people at the top"* "The best firm I have worked for"

The survey instrument is designed to obtain an individual's specific opinions about various aspects of the job, including assigned tasks, remuneration, personal growth, relationships with superiors and co-workers, and the organization. As the opinions are the concrete expressions of an individual's feelings on given issues that develop from his own personal value system (i.e. a set of things that a person consciously or subconsciously desires, wants, or seeks to attain), it may be contested that our survey instrument will not measure the degree of his job satisfaction (i.e. the internal affective evaluation of the job). However, there is evidence to suggest a close relationship between the value system and job satisfaction. Blood explained a consistent relationship between the two by presenting evidence that job satisfaction variance controlled by a personal value is independent of other variables [28]. Schaffer also argued that the more important or intensive a personal value involved, the greater the effect on job satisfaction [29]. In any case, the survey instrument that we adopted for this study should be able to measure either directly or indirectly the job satisfaction of our respondents.

FINDINGS FROM THE SURVEY

The mean Job Satisfaction (JS) scores of the Japanese subsidiary in Singapore turned out to be consistently higher, in all categories, than those obtained by its Hong Kong counterpart. Still, a striking similarity was found in the ranking order of the mean JS scores. In both cases, the local employees appear to be most satisfied with interpersonal relationships with the superior and co-workers, somewhat less satisfied with the company as a whole and job itself, and least satisfied with opportunities for promotion and present pay. The overwhelming majority of the respondents in both Hong Kong and Singapore stated that their immediate superior stood up for them and he was accessible to discuss any problems with them. Opinions about their co-workers were also very favorable, considering them as pleasant and clever people who can work well as a group.

The employees appear to be quite proud of the company they work for, as indicated by their favorable opinions about the company's reputation (63 per cent in Hong Kong, 90 per cent in Singapore) and by a strong sense of belonging (63 per cent in Hong Kong, 85 per cent in Singapore). On the negative side, however, a fair number of the respondents stated that there was too much class distinction and the company needed some fresh people at the top. Although the majority stated that the job was routine and endless, a surprising number of them still said that it was the right sort of job for them (63 per cent in Hong Kong, 90 per cent in Singapore) and it was satisfying (50 per cent in Hong Kong, 80 per cent in Singapore).

The large majority of respondents, particularly those in Hong Kong (85 per cent), stated that promotions were hard to get. Yet, 80 to 90 per cent of them felt that what they were doing was not a dead-end job and their work experience would somehow increase their prospect for promotion. It is a well-known fact that the sales personnel in retail stores, including those working at some of the larger outlets, earn very low pay; and, therefore, it is not surprising that our respondents are least satisfied with their present pay. Nonetheless, they seem to be rather resigned to this fact; nearly half the respondents in Hong Kong and three quarters in Singapore stated that their pay was fairly satisfactory.

A separate survey of 178 sales personnel at another Japanese department-store in Hong Kong supports our own survey findings [30]. Using the identical survey instrument, it has produced a similar ranking order of the mean job satisfaction scores. Table 7-5 shows the summary of findings from this and our own surveys, conducted at three different locations. At all locations, the employees are most satisfied with the factors which are inter-personal in nature; their opinions of the company are also quite favorable. On the other hand, they appear to be least satisfied with pay. In fact, they are not altogether satisfied with the factors such as challenging work and opportunities for promotion as well as financial rewards.

The top three factors, listed in Table 7-5, are generally considered by workers in Japan as relatively more important than the bottom three factors; and Japanese management tends to regard the former as motivating factors. On the basis of our survey findings, therefore, it might be concluded that the management of Japanese subsidiaries in Hong Kong and Singapore is doing a good job, in the sense of providing just the sort of motivators that count for much in generating the feeling of satisfaction among workers "in Japan". However, as discussed earlier, workers in Hong Kong or Singapore stress personal success, especially in terms of financial rewards, over social and security needs. And the local employees of the Japanese department-store are, in fact, satisfied the least with these very factors that really motivate them to work.

Table 7-5: Ranking Order of Mean Job
            Satisfaction Scores

Category	Department-store A Hong Kong	Singapore	Department-store B Hong Kong
Superior	1	1	1
Co-workers	2	2	2
Company	4	3	3
Job	3	4	5
Promotion	5	5	4
Pay	6	6	6

In other words, there exists a serious mismatch between the management and employees in their ranking order and classification of the needs. In this sense, then, the Japanese management is doing a very poor job. Perhaps, such a mismatch could explain a high employee turnover and lack of loyalty to the company among their employees - the two most serious problems that were cited by the General Managers of the Japanese subsidiaries in Hong Kong and Singapore. Good social aspects of the job or job security are not simply good enough. The local

169

employees will leave the company for a job that pays more and provides better promotion opportunities and greater challenge at work.

TOWARD A BENEVOLENT CYCLE OF BEHAVIOR

Western culture separates man's personal life from his institutional life. Western companies lay claim to mind and body, but they are culturally discouraged from intruding upon their employees' personal lives. As a result, they tend to rate employees solely on their performance at work and believe that personal matters should be left at home. By contrast, the Japanese culture integrates man's personal and institutional lives. Japanese companies believe that they have to take the whole person into account and constantly ask themselves, "Are our employees happy?" [31] To be sure, this is an important question that the management must address itself to, regardless of the culture in which the company operates.

The management should also bear in mind that motivation and satisfaction are two essential ingredients of the employees' happiness. In fact, one of the important and universal functions of management is to create and maintain an environment in which their employees are motivated to work in groups toward the accomplishment of a common objective and, at the end, they can together experience the contentment. The failure to perform this function on the part of management will create an environment in which the employees become more concerned with hygiene factors, whose presence will neither drive them toward a desired outcome nor yield the real sense of job satisfaction.

In his study at Texas Instruments, Myers found that those who sought opportunities for achievement and responsibility ("growth seekers") were concerned with motivating factors and relatively little with hygiene factors [32]. By contrast, people, characterized as "maintenance seekers", were mostly concerned with hygiene factors and relatively little with motivating factors. Moreover, Myers found that if growth seekers were treated like maintenance seekers, they soon developed the characteristics and concerns of this latter group. In short, if the right sort of opportunities was not given to the growth seekers, they would soon become the maintenance seekers. This points to a self-fulfilling prophecy.

McGregor explains the prophecy as follows [33]. "Theory X" managers do not trust their subordinates as self-motivated workers. This leads to the subordinates' irresponsible behavior, which in turn reinforces the manager's belief that employees cannot be trusted - a vicious cylcle and a self-fulfilling prophecy. "Theory Y" managers assume that people are fundamentally self-motivated and trust their subordinates. Realizing that the manager trusts them, subordinates actually do the best they can, which in turn reinforces the manager's original beliefs and behavior - a self-fulfilling prophecy again but this time a more benevolent cycle.

Our study has indicated that workers in Hong Kong or Singapore, at all levels, are more of the growth seeker than the mere maintenance seeker. They must, therefore, be trusted and treated as people who are motivated by higher needs for achievement, recognition, and advancement as well as monetary rewards. Highly motivated workers with low job satisfaction will look for new jobs in different organizations, leaving behind those who might only be considered as losers. In order to retain a happy work-force of winners loyal to the company, who are highly motivated and satisfied to contribute to the company's success, it would seem essential for the management of Japanese subsidiaries operating in East Asia to start paying much closer attention to the culture-specific motivating factors for their non-Japanese employees.

NOTES

1. McGregor, D., The Human Side of Enterprise, New York: McGraw-Hill, (1960)
2. Likert, R., The Human Organization, New York: McGraw-Hill, (1967)
3. Deese, J., Principles of Psychology, Boston: Allyn & Bacon, (1964), p.54
4. Skinner, B.F., Beyond Freedom and Dignity, New York: Alfred A. Knopf, (1971)

5. Campbell, J.P., M.D. Dunnette, E.E. Lawler, III and K.E. Weick, Jr., Managerial Behavior, Performance, and Effectiveness, New York: McGraw-Hill, (1970)

6. Maslow, A.H., "A Theory of Human Motivation", Psychological Review, (Jul. 1943), pp. 370-396

7. Reitz, H.J., "The Relative Importance of Five Categories of Needs among Individual Workers in Eight Countries", Proceedings of the Academy of Management Conference, (1975), pp.270-273

8. O'Reilly, C.A. and K.H. Roberts, "Job Satisfaction among Whites and Non-Whites", Journal of Applied Psychology, (1973), vol.57, no.3, pp.295-299

9. Hofstede, G., "Motivation, Leadership, and Organization: Do American Theories Apply Abroad?", Organizational Dynamics, (summer 1980), pp.42-43

10. Sirota, D. and M.J. Greenwood, "Understanding Your Overseas Workforce", Harvard Business Review (Jan./Feb. 1971), pp.53-60

11. Herzberg, F., Work and the Nature of Man, Cleveland, OH: The World Publishing Co., (1966)

12. Hines, G.H., "Achievement, Motivation, Occupations and Labor Turnover in New Zealand", Journal of Applied Psychology, (1973), vol.58, no.3, pp.313-319

13. Vroom, V.H., Work and Motivation, New York: John Wiley & Sons, (1964)

14. Adler, N.J., International Dimensions of Organizational Behavior, Boston: Kent Publishing Co., (1986)

15. Matsui, T. and I. Terai, "A Cross-Cultural Study of the Validity of the Expectancy Theory of Work Motivation", Journal of Applied Psychology, (1979), vol.60, no.2, pp.263-265

16. Hofstede, G., (1980), op.cit.

17. Graham, R.G. and K. Leung, "Management Motivation in Hong Kong", The Hong Kong Manager, (Feb./Mar. 1987), pp.17-24

18. Lau, C.M., "A Survey of Job Value Systems Among Business Students", working paper #8, Department of Business & Management, City Polytechnic of Hong Kong, (Apr. 1986)

19. Lam, M.Y., "The Reassessment of Japanese Practices of Management in Hong Kong", project report, Department of Business & Management, City Polytechnic of Hong Kong, (May 1987)

20. Hofstede, G., _Culture's Consequences: International Differences in Work-related Values_, Beverly Hills, CA: Sage Publications, (1984)

21. Robins, S., _Organization Behavior_, Englewood Cliffs, NJ: Prentice-Hall, (1986)

22. Inglehart, R., _Changing Values and Political Style among Western Publics_, Princeton, NJ: Princeton University Press, (1971)

23. Graham, R.G. and K. Leung, (1987), op.cit.

24. Li, P.K., "To What Extent is Japanese-style Management Transplanted in Japanese Subsidiaries in Hong Kong? - A Case Study", project report, Department of Business & Management, City Polytechnic of Hong Kong, (May 1987)

25. Newstram, J. et al, "Motivating the Public Employees: Facts versus Fiction", _Public Personnel Management_, (Jan./Feb. 1976), pp. 67-72; Herzberg, F., "Motivation, Moral, and Money", _Psychology Today_, (Mar. 1968), p.66

26. Kast, F.E. and J.E. Rosenzweig, _Organization and Management: A Systems and Contingency Approach_, New York: McGraw Hill, (1982)

27. Cook, J.D. et al, _The Experience of Work: A Compendium and Review of 249 Measures and Their Use_, New York: Academic Press, (1981), pp.61-63

28. Blood, M.R., "Work Values and Job Satisfaction", _Journal of Applied Psychology_, (1969), pp.456-459

29. Schaffer, R.H., "Job Satisfaction as Related to Need Satisfaction in Work", _Psychological Monograph_, (1953)

30. Li, P.K., (1987), op.cit.

31. Johnson, R.T. and W.G. Ouchi, "Made in America (under Japanese Management)", _Harvard Business Review_, (Sept./Oct. 1976), pp.61-69

32. Myers, M.S., "Who are Your Motivated Workers?", _Harvard Business Review_, (Jan./Feb. 1964), pp.73-86

33. McGregor, D., (1960), op.cit.

Chapter Eight

CONCLUSION:
IS JAPANESE-STYLE MANAGEMENT TRANSFERABLE?

Many observers of Japanese business have attributed Japan's post-War economic miracle to the country's success in achieving the world's highest productivity through the effective human resource management (HRM). Japanese HRM is firmly based on the people-oriented philosophy which believes that people are the most important of all organizational resources. This philosophy is well reflected in the community-oriented ideology adopted by Japanese companies, which stresses total concern for people. The company thus concerns itself with the private life of its employees as well as their performance at work. Such a philosophy underpins Japanese corporate culture, and it undoubtedly influences the practices of management. Can Japanese-style management, which incorporates the culture with the practices, be successfully transferred abroad? In this final chapter, the question of transferability will be addressed first by examining views held by Japanese managers, who are stationed in East Asia, and their actions as observed in the actual employment of the features of Japanese-style management. Relationships between management practices, management effectiveness, and enterprise effectiveness will then be re-examined to determine what we can really learn from the Japanese.

ATTRIBUTE OF JAPAN'S ECONOMIC SUCCESS

Before 1950, "Made in Japan" goods had earned around the world a reputation for being shoddy and cheap. However, over the last thirty-seven years, that tarnished image has been fast replaced with one of high quality and dependability. And, by 1985, Japan accounted for 10 per cent of world exports, equalling the US as the world's biggest exporter [1]. What happened back in 1950? The answer is that the Japanese became convinced that quality was vital for export and that they could make the switch. Since then, they have been striving to improve quality, decrease costs, and capture markets the world over with better quality and lower prices.

Folklore has it that quality and productivity are incompatible. You cannot have both - it is either or. If one pushes quality, the productivity falls; if one pushes produc- tivity, the quality suffers. Yet, Japan has succeeded to achieve both quality and produc- tivity. During a seven-year period between 1979 and 1986, Japan's manufacturing productivity grew at the annual rate of nearly 6 per cent (3.5 per cent in the US, 3 per cent in West Germany), making her the world productivity leader [2]. Deming, who is generally regarded as the father of the modern quality control movement, believes that this very achievement holds a key for Japan's extraordinary success in developing a huge export-driven economy in the post-War period [3].

Historically, the largest increases in productivity have occurred because more and better machinery (i.e. capital) was introduced by management in the capital-labor mix. And Japan's high productivity has no doubt resulted from her high capital investment. However, in recent years, the economists in the US came up with an important finding that scarcely half the increase in productivity can be accounted for by the increase in capital itself; at least half the increase in productivity is a residual that seems to be attributable to scientific and engineering advance, to industrial improvement and, above all, to the knowhow of management methods and educational training of labor [4]. Though it is difficult to separate capital formation and technology completely, a shift of focus from capital to residuals of technology such as management knowhow and manpower training as an important attribute of productivity is significant.

Of a variety of approaches used today to boost productivity, an employee participation program is generally considered as the most effective. Other useful measures include better

175

communication, better labor-management relations, and increased training, which all encompass the management of people. At the conclusion of their paper published in 1984, Petty, McGee and Cavender stated [5]:

> Recent public policy discussions have emphasized macro economic strategies for improving labor productivity in the US. Incentives for capital investment and research and development are important, but the results of the present study support the development of more effective human resource management policies.
> [Petty, M.M., G.W. McGee, and J.W. Cavender, 1984, p.720]

In a management classic "The Practice of Management" written more than 30 years ago, Peter Drucker pointed out that one of the most important functions of management is to make a productive enterprise out of human resources - not from an inanimate resource such as capital [6]. Productivity means the balance between all factors of production that will give the greatest output for the smallest input. Higher productivity implies better utilization of resources. Drucker maintains that man, alone of all the resources, can grow and develop; other resources can be better or worse utilized, but they can never produce an output greater than the sum of inputs. People are thus the primary source of productivity gains. He cautions, however, that human resources must be considered as human-beings who require, among other things, motivation and satisfaction. And it is management, and management alone, that can satisfy all these requirements.

More recently, Peters and Waterman's study of America's best-run companies came up with a list of eight attributes of excellence, that included "productivity through people" [7]. The study revealed that the successful companies treated people, not the capital, as the primary source of productivity gains. In short, these companies treat all employees as their most important asset and, moreover, treat them with dignity and repect, making everyone feel that their work counts toward higher productivity and the financial reward that goes with it. The point, then, is the completeness of the people-orientation in the excellent companies.

For example, IBM, perhaps one of the biggest and oldest American companies practicing the people-orientation, has the corporate philosophy that starts with respect for the individual. This is a simple concept. But at IBM it occupies a major portion of management time, and the managers devote more effort to it than anything else, as well reflected in such practices as life-time employment, the open-door policy, promotion from within, IBM country club, IBM day-care centers, IBM hotels, monthly opinion surveys by the personnel department, and the intense training. The people-orientation is also complete at Hewlett-Packard (HP), whose statement of corporate philosophy starts with the sentence that reads: "The achievements of an organization are the results of the combined efforts of each individual." The company calls its people-oriented philosophy the HP Way, which emphasizes the dignity and worth of the individual. At both IBM and HP, the concern for people is considered essential to enhance productivity. This concern is more than a matter of policy; it is a philosophy.

Many researchers feel that studying the productivity gap would contribute to explaining Japan's relative success compared with other developed countries in the West. Their studies have led to the hypothesis that the Japanese have evolved human resource management (HRM) practices that are particularly effective in achieving high productivity [8]. The most popular of these practices include collective decision-making by consensus, group duties and responsibilities, the life-time employment system, comprehensive welfare program, seniority-based pay system, seniority-based promotion system, on-the-job training, and job rotation. These practices are assumed to create a strong commitment to work, engender a strong motivation to contribute to the success of the company, and instil a strong sense of job satisfaction in the typical Japanese worker. To be sure, Japanese HRM practices are supported by the management ideologies which stress group harmony and total concern for people. Together, these group-oriented and community-oriented ideologies constitute the corporate culture of the typical Japanese company. Corporate culture is an integral part of organizational life, and has important implications for the practices of management.

Can the corporate culture and management practices typically adopted by Japanese companies be successfully transplanted on a foreign soil to generate strong job satisfaction and high productivity among local employees working for Japanese companies abroad? A conviction, or a lack of it, about their transferability on the part of Japanese managers could have a significant influence on the actual employment of the features of Japanese-style management.

VIEWS ON MANAGEMENT TRANSFERABILITY

In chapter six, we examined the extent of the employment of the features of Japanese-style management (i.e. ideologies and practices) in more than one hundred Japanese subsidiaries operating in Hong Kong and Singapore. On the basis of the scores obtained, the sample firms could be divided into three groups - Type X, Y and Z. Type X companies employ the features of Japanese-style management to the greatest extent, whereas Type Z companies employ them to the least extent. Seventeen per cent of the Japanese subsidiaries in Hong Kong belong to Type X, 58 per cent to Type Y and the rest (25 per cent) to Type Z. A breakdown in Singapore is 7 per cent, 51 percent and 42 per cent, respectively. It is quite clear that in both countries, a majority of the companies employ the features of Japanese-style management only to a moderate extent.

When asked to state their view on the transferability of Japanese-style management, only a little over 10 per cent of the companies in either Hong Kong or Singapore expressed a strong conviction that it could be transferred. As shown in Table 8-1, there are significantly more companies that have a negative feeling about transferability. And, the majority remains uncertain, expressing neither a very positive nor a very negative view.

Table 8-1: Views on the Transferability of
         Japanese-style Management

Type	Transfer of Japanese-style Management							
	"Possible"		"?"		"Impossible"		Total	
	HK	SGR	HK	SGR	HK	SGR	HK	SGR
X	5	2	6	1	0	0	11 (17%)	3 (7%)
Y	4	2	26	15	9	5	39 (58%)	22 (51%)
Z	0	1	12	7	5	10	17 (25%)	18 (42%)
Total	9 (13%)	5 (12%)	44 (66%)	23 (53%)	14 (21%)	15 (35%)	67	43

Note: HK=Hong Kong, SGR=Singapore

There is some correlation between the expressed view and the action actually taken. For one, there is not a single company that has a totally negative view (i.e. "impossible") and yet employs the features of Japanese-style management to a large extent (i.e. "Type X" company). The reverse is also true, with just one exception in Singapore. The largest number of companies (39 per cent and 35 per cent in Hong Kong and Singapore, respectively) is uncertain about the transferability and, in fact, employ Japanese-style management only to a moderate extent. Still there is a clear indication that the more positive the expressed view, the greater the employment of the features of Japanese-style management.

We must note, however, there were considerable variations in the actual extent of employment even within a group of companies with the same view. Such variations were most evident within the group of Japanese subsidiaries in Singapore which expressed a strong positive view on transferability. As a matter of fact, there were more variations in the extent of employment as the group's view became more positive.

APPROACHES IN MANAGEMENT TRANSFER

In their study of Japanese subsidiaries operating in the US, Sethi and his associates classified the companies into four distinctive groups based on their approaches in applying Japanese-style management [9]:

Type A Companies - The Imperialist Approach
Type B Companies - The Enclave Approach
Type C Companies - The Domestication Approach
Type D Companies - The Accultural Approach

Type A companies are among the most tradition-bound in Japan; they have vast networks of international operations but are primarily focused in Japan; they consist mostly of large trading houses such as Mitsui, Sumitomo and C.Itoh. Type B companies are generally small in size, and both the number of total employees and the ratio of Japanese to local employees are relatively small; they set up operations in fairly small and isolated parts of the country. Type C companies, which include the electronics giants such as Matsushita, Sony and Sharp are generally in the high technology area, operate in tight labor markets and need highly skilled people. Type D companies are at the forefront of the Japanese companies which have developed highly automated and integrated manufacturing systems; not only do they bring in their management philosophy, they also transplant intact their manufacturing process; this group consists mostly of large auto-makers such as Honda and Nissan.

Perhaps, differences among the four types of companies could be best understood by comparing Type A and Type D companies (see Table 8-2). In the case of Type A companies, the application of Japanese-style management to the locals tends to be indifferent, incidental and often forced. By contrast, the approach taken by Type D companies is that of fair, planned and cultivated application of Japanese-style management [10]. In the main, in treating their local workers, Type A companies employ a "2-Class System", whereas Type D companies employ a "1-Class System". In between, there are companies employing what I might call a "1.5-Class System".

Table 8-2: Application of Japanese-style
Management ("Type A" versus "Type D")

Type A	Type D
Skeptical that its own corporate culture and management practices can be transplanted on a foreign soil.	Convinced that its own corporate culture and management practices can be transplanted on a foreign soil.
Maintain the purity of the culture by limiting its application only to the Japanese; treat the natives according to the customs of the local society.	Purify the natives by absorbing them into the culture; if necessary, create a new culture where both Japanese and local workers will share a common set of values.
Operate two somewhat different systems for Japanese and local workers. (Exclusion of the locals from the system; "2-Class System")	Operate one and the same system for Japanese and local workers. (Integration of the locals into the system; "1-Class System")

As pointed out earlier, only about one out of every ten Japanese subsidiaries in Hong Kong or Singapore has a strong conviction about the transferability of Japanese-style management. In this case, then, could we say that the Japanese companies operating in East Asia are attempting to maintain the purity of their own corporate culture and management practices by limiting their application only to the Japanese? In short, are they in fact operating two different systems for the Japanese and the locals? Answers to these questions might be found by examining the way local workers are treated.

Provided with explanations about the two sharply contrasting approaches in treating local employees (i.e. "1-Class System" versus "2-Class System"), the personnel managers of 110 sample firms from Hong Kong and Singapore were asked to indicate which approach was actually taken by their companies. As shown in Table 8-3, the companies which have adopted the "2-Class System" (i.e. "Type A companies") form a very small minority in either Hong Kong or Singapore. Though the number of companies which have adopted the "1-Class System" (i.e. "Type D companies") is relatively larger, particularly in Hong Kong, the vast majority (around 80 per cent) appears to have adopted the "1.5-Class System". In other words, regardless of the industry they are in, most Japanese companies operating in these two countries neither exclude local workers entirely from the system nor integrate them fully into the system. The treatment of local workers could only be regarded as fair.

Table 8-3: Treatment of Local Workers

	Hong Kong	Singapore
2-Class System	3 (4%)	3 (7%)
1.5-Class System	52 (78%)	36 (84%)
1-Class system	12 (18%)	4 (9%)
Total	67 (100%)	43 (100%)

What are the implications of the way, in which the locals are treated, for job satisfaction? To examine this, let us take another look at the findings from the Worker Opinion Survey conducted at two branches of a major Japanese department store - one in Hong Kong and another in Singapore. The two Japanese subsidiaries under study belong to a minority group in each respective country of operations in that their management has expressed an entirely positive view on the transferability of Japanese-style management and that they are both employing the features of Japanese-style management to a relatively large extent. On the other hand, they are different from each other in the treatment of local employees. Whereas the Hong Kong branch appears to have adopted the "1.5-Class System", the Singapore branch has adopted the "1-Class System".

As noted in the previous chapter, local employees at the Singapore branch have shown a higher satisfaction with each and every work-related factor included in our study (i.e. superior, co-workers, company, job itself, promotion, pay). Being the subsidiaries of the same company from Japan, the human resource management policies at these two overseas branches are more or less the same. However, their approaches in treating the locals are different, and the degree of class distinction within the organization would seem to have influenced the local employees' satisfaction with the company. As a consequence of adopting the "1-Class System", which attempts to integrate the local workers into the system, the Singapore branch indeed conducts in-company training on a larger scale than the Hong Kong branch does. This, in turn, could have possibly resulted in their employees' greater satisfaction with the job itself, opportunities for promotion and pay, which had been identified as the real motivating factors in the sense of yielding a feeling of satisfaction among workers in Singapore as well as in Hong Kong. In essence, the gap in the local employees' job satisfaction could be explained, in large part, by a somewhat different application of the community-oriented ideology of management to practices, as is evident in different approaches in treating the local employees.

JOB SATISFACTION AND PRODUCTIVITY

It is often assumed that it is the Japanese human resource management practices per se that generate the employees' strong work commitment, high motivation and satisfaction. However, this causal attribution may be misleading. Causal influence might flow in the opposite direction. In other words, the practices are effective because employees are committed to work, self-motivated, and are able to find job satisfation themselves. Although their interests might have changed over the years, the Japanese instinctive interest in work has remained more or less intact.

Japanese managers believe in the innate ability of the individual to confer meaning on work even in the absence of strong stimuli from the environment; and many have even tried to convince the non-Japanese local employees that they must play a critical role themselves in determining the meaning of work. There is little doubt that such a belief has been accumulated over time through their experience in Japan. And it is mostly based on the facts obtained through their observations of the Japanese workers. However, given the different socio-cultural backgrounds, it is not surprising that they have more often than not failed to convince the local employees to accept the Japanese view on the meaning of work.

It is quite clear that the practices of Japanese-style management, which appear to be effective in creating work motivation and job satisfaction for employees at home, cannot be successfully transferred without the creation of the conditions that have nurtured them. One of these conditions is the Japanese view on the meaning of work. It could be said that the ability of the Japanese employees to confer meaning on work is not innate but has been mostly learned from other individuals and groups in Japan. An implication is that such an ability could also be taught to the non-Japanese employees through more extensive and intensive in-house training and development programs, which are at present very much neglected as noted in our survey conducted in Hong Kong and Singapore. Until a new culture, where both Japanese and local employees are treated as equal to share a common set of values, is created, it is doubtful whether the Japanese HRM practices can become truly effective in generating enhanced job satisfaction for non-Japanese workers.

The culture of a particular organization is the set of understandings that the members of the organization share in common, and consists of norms, attitudes, values, and beliefs. It may be inferred from the things, sayings, doings, and feelings held in common [11]. For example, a shared understanding on the perception of the company as part of the family may be gauged by the existence of shared feelings such as "the company is good to us", "we like this place", and "we care about this company because it cares about us as individuals."

In general, the community-oriented ideology of Japanese management reflecting such a shared understanding seems to be well appreciated by local workers in both Hong Kong and Singapore, as is evident in a high level of satisfaction with the company. Japanese corporate culture is also expressed in the group-oriented ideology, which emphasizes the harmony. It appears that the group-oriented ideology is even more appreciated by the local workers, as is evident in a relatively higher level of satisfaction with the superior and co-workers. However, this same ideology and the practices of management, influenced by the ideology, would seem to have had quite a contrary effect on satisfaction with the job itself, promotion and pay due to a diffusion of duties/responsibilities and a loss of identity as an individual.

Job satisfaction is often treated as an intervening variable between management practices and productivity. However, the nature of relationships between employees' job satisfaction and their productivity remains unclear. There are three major viewpoints that have been assumed by organizational theorists with respect to the satisfaction-productivity relationships [12]:

* Satisfaction causes productivity
* Productivity causes satisfaction
* The satisfaction-productivity relationship is moderated by a number of other variables (e.g. pressure for production, occupational group, degree of job fit, job level, rewards)

Empirical supports for each of the viewpoints listed above have been weak, casting doubt about their validity. That workers are satisfied does not necessarily mean that they will produce more; the reverse may also be true. The moderator approach has also failed to produce unambiguous and reliable findings. Perhaps, we can only conclude that:

* The practices-satisfaction relationship is circular, with the view on the meaning of work playing an important role.
* The satisfaction-productivity relationship is circular, with some variables acting as the moderator.

Figure 8-1: Modified Model of Comparative
           Management

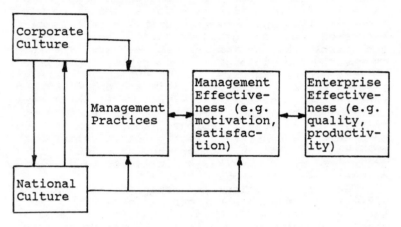

The comparative management model, which we
have proposed in chapter two (see Figure 2-4),
indicates the influence of corporate culture and
national culture on management practices. It
also suggests causal relationships between
management practices, management effectiveness,
and enterprise effectiveness. On the basis of
discussions above, however, it would seem
necessary to modify the originally-proposed model
of comparative management as shown in Figure 8-1.

DEMYSTIFYING JAPANESE-STYLE MANAGEMENT

Following the rapid rise of the yen and a slow-
down in economic growth, Japanese-style
management today is under pressure. While most
companies still retain the people-orientation
that is the heart of the Japanese human resource
management, many have been forced to diverge and
sacrifice long-standing practices such as
lifetime employment and the seniority-based pay
system. The result is a declining loyalty to the
company as well as a deterioration in job
satisfaction among Japanese workers.

As early as 1983, a Gallup poll sponsored by
the Japanese government showed that contrary to a
long-held myth, workers in Japan as a whole and
the younger workers in particular were less
relaxed and much less satisfied with their jobs

than American or European workers. A more recent survey of workers in ten countries confirmed this finding [13]. Among twenty work-related factors examined in the study, only three received a favorable response from the majority of over 3,000 Japanese workers who participated in the survey. They were relationships with co-workers, health and safety, and security of employment. It is to be noted that even the security of employment, offered through the life-time employment system, is a realistic prospect for at most 25 per cent of workers in Japan; it is something which is only enjoyed by male employees working for large companies. On the other hand, more than 80 per cent of the workers expressed dissatisfaction with participation in decision-making, pay and fringe benefits, and promotion opportunities. It is significant that in expressing their satisfaction or dissatisfaction, Japanese workers are quite similar after all to their counterparts in East Asia, who were the samples in our Worker Opinion Survey.

Quite possibly, the low level of satisfaction among Japanese workers reflects their high expectations. According to Vroom's Expectancy Theory, people will be motivated to do things to the extent of expectation that their action will help them achieve desired results [14]. Japanese workers' high expectations will thus present a serious problem to the management in motivating and satisfying their employees. Such a problem is especially acute in dealing with working women in Japan's male-oriented companies. Nearly half the working women in Tokyo are dissatisfied with their jobs, according to a recent survey, and more than half have thought about quitting to find new ones [15]. Both statistics reflect an evolution in the Japanese work ethic.

Because of a homogeneous corporate culture and a high congruence of individual goals and organizational goals, it is believed that Japanese employees expend more energy on their work than their Western counterparts [16]. According to a survey conducted in 1985 by the Ministry of Labor, Japan was the only developed country where the industrial worker put in more than 2,000 hours a year to work. On the average, the Japanese worked 2,168 hours, including 221 hours of overtime (UK-1938, US-1898, France-1657,

187

West Germany-1613). However, a new breed of Japanese workers today are demanding shorter working hours in order to start enjoying the fruit of the country's economic success outside the company. There is a new realization among them that the time has come for the development of new culture, in which everyone should be able to set his own objectives and have the satisfaction of pursuing goals that he, rather than the group, has set for himself. A 1980 government poll of people aged between 15 and 19 revealed that more than 71 per cent of the youngsters craved an individual life-style and only a little over 9 per cent desired to lead lives useful to the society or the company.

Though the evolution in the Japanese work ethic may be slow, a new generation of youth, both men and women, in Japan are no longer bound by the life-time employment system. They seek a job, not a company; they want to work someplace where they can fully exhibit their skills. As the economic feasibility of life-time employment is being questioned, more Japanese companies are also finding that it pays to reward performance instead of tenure. With job-hopping gradually losing its stigma, some companies have begun to pay top wages to workers with the right skills rather than losing them to competitors.

A strong uneasiness prevails among the public in Japan that their country will become isolated in the international community as a result of mounting foreign dissatisfaction over its huge trade imbalance. However, the white paper on the economy for fiscal 1987 issued by the Economic Planning Agency states that the economy has become less dependent on exports, with economic growth relying more on an expansion in domestic demand. The cautiously optimistic report concludes that the restructuring of the economy into one more harmonious with the rest of the world must be implemented without hurting the solidarity of Japanese society.

Today there is also a growing awareness in the Japanese business circle that their management practices at home may need major adjustments if the country is to maintain its edge over other industrialized countries in the West. In fact, some of the traditional Japanese-style management practices are changing due mainly to the on-going structural change of the economy and the internationalization of business. The life-time employment system and seniority-based pay system, for example, are gradually taking on the form of American and Western models under the mounting pressure from within and outside Japan. According to the Ministry of International Trade and Industry, some 700,000 people are now working overseas for Japanese companies. As more and more companies set up overseas operations, Japanese managers are becoming increasingly aware of the need for adjustments to the practices of the home-grown management abroad as well.

LESSONS FROM JAPAN

Throughout their history, the Japanese have been extremely successful in coping with tough challenges coming from outside their country, often by force and surprise. They have somehow managed to turn them into opportunities for devising something better. Some 150 years after the American Commodore Mathew Perry arrived in his "black ship" to force open feudal Japan to the rest of the world, President Ronald Reagan of the US is now demanding the further opening of Japan's domestic market to the West. Japan today is bracing herself to meet this latest challenge through the bold restructuring of the economy and and the rapid internationalization of business. To succeed, the Japanese have stepped up the process of learning from others, as they have always done.

The Japanese are said to have a good eye for spotting the germ of a foregin idea and the brain to grow it into something useful in their country. It could be argued that Japan's economic success to date has, in large part, been achieved upon efficient borrowing and ingenious adaptation. In fact, most of the characteristics of Japanese management were formulated after World War II, and many of them were transplanted from the West. The so-called examples of successful Japanese management methods and techniques had been developed in the industrialized West long before Japanese management became fashionable, even to the surprise of many Japanese. It can be said that the particular strength of Japanese management is its ability to recognize changing environmental factors and its courage in abandoning old conventions when they are no

longer appropriate or useful. In fact, the
Japanese have neither pretended nor claimed to be
the original developer of modern management
concepts and knowhow.

Until as recently as 1980, Japanese
management was seen by many as the answer to
Western industry's ills. It is also seen by some
East Asian countries as the quick answer to
emulate Japan's economic success. However, many
people have found that imitating the Japanese in
gimmic-laden fashion will not lead to a success.
Clark, for one, believes that the success of the
Japanese enterprise is solely due to its people,
who are able to confer the meaning on work
themselves [17]. Having got over the Japanese
management fad, some managers in the West today
even admit that they have become lazy, lacking
the resolution to do the things they know need to
be done - the discipline, the hard work, the
sound definition of tough goals, and self-control
to achieve them. These managers believe that if
they can copy that aspect of Japanese management,
they will not need any other kinds of imitation
[18].

It is quite clear that the West of the 19th
century and thereafter did not provide a
completely transferable model for the modernization to Japan. In a similar fashion, the
factors of Japan's success in achieving economic
superpower status may not always be adopted in
other countries. In the late 1960s, the Japanese
consciously decided to hold onto their
distinctive model. Similarly, those in the West
today seem to be looking to an appropriate model
of their own rather than to the Japanese. For
years, the traditional inclination of the
Westerners to conceive their society as a model
for all others, combined with the special blind
spots in Western thoughts about Japan, has led to
the treatment of Japanese management with a
mixture of arrogance and disregard. In the
complex interaction between Japan and the West
over the past forty years, it is clearly the
Japanese who have benefited more. And they have
done so essentially because so many of them have
observed the West in minute detail.

What can we really learn from the Japanese?
In a number of instances, the Japanese have been
able to successfully apply their style of
management abroad. One such example is the
application of the community-oriented ideology,

leading to a relatively high satisfaction with the company among local employees working for Japanese companies. Other evidence, however, indicates many problems emerging in this process. Examples of problems are inadequate financial rewards, a lack of promotion opportunities, and less satisfaction with the job itself. To be sure, these problems do not seem to be only limited to non-Japanese local employees but also prevail today among Japanese employees in the home land. This mixed picture should give us a clear warning against simplistic thinking regarding the transferability of Japanese-style management.

The primary commitment of the Japanese has long been to the well-being of the various groups to which they belong - family, clan, company, country, and so on - rather than to an individual ideology or religion; and racially and culturally, Japan is perhaps the most homogeneous of the world's nations. As a result, the Japanese have been able to readily accept changes for the good of the group, yet still preserving a keen sense of special identity. The Japanese have been learning with all eagerness what they consider better than their own from other countries. They have been applying what they have learned to their needs and objectives, and have then gone on to adapt creatively using their own resources and capabilities. In the process of adaptation, they have made a clear distinction between the borrowed and the native. Quite possibly, such a creative adaptation is the most important lesson that others could learn from the Japanese.

The "Japanization" of Quality Circles (QCs) - the concept imported from the US in the 1950s - has greatly helped many Japanese companies achieve high product quality and labor productivity at the same time. It has become so successful that many Americans even believe that QCs were invented in a culture vastly different from theirs and, therefore, are not culturally suited to them. The search for new and effective practices of management is common to all companies and countries in this era of the increasing internationalization of business and rapid environmental changes. There is really no reason why managers in other countries cannot do what the Japanese have been doing to find useful concepts and knowhow of management, even from countries which are very different in culture from their own.

Given a commonality in the cultural tradition, it might be argued that the practices of Japanese management can be more readily transferred to East Asia than to the West. And such transfer may prove to be useful as well. In fact, there is some evidence that suggests that Japanese companies in East Asia are taking more positive steps to Japanize local operations than their counterparts operating in the West [19]. However, our study has revealed that Japanese managers working in East Asia remain rather skeptical about the transferability of their home-grown style of management even to their neighboring countries with similar cultural backgrounds. Their view is not very different after all from the one generally held by their counterparts working in the US or Western Europe.

In other words, regardless of the geographical locations of operations, Japanese companies remain extremely cautious, and have not come to the point of adopting all the features of their traditional management style. They have indeed adopted, to a considerable degree, the host-country practices which are different from their own, sometimes to a marked degree. It seems that a modified Japanese-style management is now emerging in various parts of the world. A close look at Japanese management practices has exposed problems and weaknesses as well as solutions and strengths. The transferability of Japanese-style management to a very different culture or, for that matter, even to a seemingly similar culture is indeed a complex issue that will require great patience and careful analysis.

NOTES

1. Business News (South China Morning Post, Dec. 20, 1985), "Japan's Per Capita GNP to Surpass US", p.3

2. Fortune International, "Productivity Perks Up", (Sept. 28, 1987), p.47

3. Deming, W.E, Out of the Crisis, Cambridge, MA: MIT Center for Advanced Engineering Study, (1986)

4. Samuelson, P., Economics, New York: McGraw Hill, (1980), p.692

5. Petty, M.M., G.W. McGee and J.W. Cavender, "A Meta-Analysis of the Relationships Between Individual Job Satisfaction and Individual Performance", Academy of Management Review, (Oct. 1984), pp.712-721

6. Drucker, P., The Practice of Management, New York: Harper & Row, (1954)

7. Peters, T.J. and R.H. Waterman, Jr., In Search of Excellence, New York: Harper & Row, (1982)

8. Campbell, D.J., "The Meaning of Work: American and Japanese Paradigms", Asia Pacific Journal of Management, (Sept. 1985), pp.1-9

9. Sethi, S.P., N. Namiki and C.L. Swanson, The False Promise of the Japanese Miracle, London: Pitman, (1984)

10. ibid.

11. Stoner, J.A.F. and C. Wankel, Management, Englewood Cliffs, NJ: Prentice-Hall, (1986)

12. Schwab, D.P. and L.L. Cummings, "Theories of Performance and Satisfaction: A Review", Industrial Relations, (1970), vol.9, pp.408-430

13. Ishikawa, A., "Interim Report of the Result of Attitude Survey of Electrical Workers in Ten Countries", mimeograph, Tokyo: Japan Federation of Electrical Trade Unions, (1985)

14. Vroom, V.H., Work and Motivation, New York: John Wiley & Sons, (1964)

15. South China Morning Post, "Nearly Half Tokyo's Office Ladies Unhappy at Work",(Jun. 24, 1987), p.15

16. Cole, R., Work Mobility and Participation, Berkeley: University of California Press, (1979)

17. Clark, G., "The People are the Enterprise", PHP, (Dec. 1981), pp.31-34 & 51-58

18. Odiorne, G.S., "The Trouble with Japanese Management System", Business Horizon, (Jun./Aug. 1984), pp.17-23

19. Ishida, H., "Transferability of Japanese Human Resource Management Abroad", Human Resource Management, (Spring 1986), pp.103-120

CHINESE MANAGEMENT:
WHATEVER HAPPENED TO ITS TRADITIONS?

The Chinese have one of the oldest continuous
civilizations in the world - going back some
4,000 years - and also the oldest centralized
bureaucratic state that has survived for well
over 2,000 years. While management, as we
understand today, is largely of Western origin, a
close examination of Chinese classics, written by
ancient China's great philosophers and military
strategists, reveals that the Chinese had in
fact laid down the solid foundation for modern
management principles centuries before management
began to be treated as a separate academic
discipline in the West. Between the 6th and 4th
centuries BC, Confucius, Han Fei Tzu, and Sun Tsu
among numerous others had taught the rulers of
their time moral principles and comprehensive
strategies, many of which are still applicable to
the the management of modern organizations. Over
the last forty years, China's government policy
and leadership, swinging from left to right and
back again like a pendulum, have changed without
resulting in any significant economic progress
for the country. Despite its time-honored
tradition in management, as perhaps best
demonstrated by the work of Ch'in Shihuang ("The
First Emperor of China"), China today is in dire
need for management reforms in order to modernize
the vast country of over 1.1 billion people.
During the past decade, China has increasingly
turned to the West for help in the area of
management, and has also begun to show a renewed
interest in its own management tradition through
the readings of selected classics. It may,
therefore, be useful to examine the current state
of management practices in China as well as the
country's drive to catch up on lost time.

DOCTRINES OF TWO GREAT SAGES

Among the philosophers of ancient China, whose teachings have greatly influenced the rulers of China to date, stand out two great sages - Confucius and Han Fei Tzu. The former founded and spread Confucianism, and the latter Legalism. Confucius taught, in the 6th century BC, five virtues of "jen" (benevolent love) and "li" (propriety) as well as "i" (righteousness), "chih" (wisdom), and "hsin" (faithfulness). The Confucian doctrine was transmitted through a great many Chinese classics. In one such classic "Analect", Confucius said, "When a prince's personal conduct is correct, his government is effective without the issuing of orders. If his personal conduct is not correct, he may issue orders but they will not be followed" [1]. To conduct oneself according to the rules of propriety or "li" in itself would give one a moral status. The Confucian doctrine of "jen" called for loving others in a graded fashion, beginning with one's own father, family, and friends; relationships thus defined were between superior and subordinate. And the bond of loyalty on the part of subordinates to the ruler was codified in "hsin". This meant the status that the ruler had earned through his proper conduct gave him a privilege to dominate others lower down in the societal hierarchy.

However, the doctrine of "i" stated that the ruled, especially the educated upper class, had a moral responsibility to speak out even against the ruler when he did not conduct himself properly. The famous Chinese maxim states that a scholar should be the first to become concerned with the world's troubles and the last to rejoice in its happiness. Chinese history has not lacked heroes who have attacked rulers in terms of principle. An underlying concept of all these virtues was that some people had more gifts than others - people were not equal in their capacity. Personal worth was not considered innate within each human soul but had to be aquired through learning (i.e. the doctrine of "chih"). To sum up, Confucius and his followers advised the rulers of China to adopt the moral principles, as expressed in the five virtues, in order to maintain harmony and order and thus keep a society together without the exercise of force.

Like Confucianism, the doctrine of Legalism also dealt with hierarchical relationships between superior and subordinate. Although Han Fei Tzu was not the founder of the legalist school of thought among the ancient Chinese philosophers, he combined the earlier works and incorporated them in a collective work in the 4th century BC. The doctrine of Legalism can be explained by two principal concepts - "fa" (rules) and "shu" (the art of governing) [2]. "Fa" referred to the system of procedures, rules, and regulations drawn up by the ruler and distributed to his subordinates for compliance. The system was backed up by punishments to be inflicted on those who did not conform and rewards to be granted to those who did. "Shu" was a set of principles and the art of governing by which the ruler exercised his authority. In other words, while subordinates were kept in line by "fa", the leader was guided by "shu". The ruler is to use both "fa" and "shu" to control the behavior of subordinates and retain his power.

Han Fei Tzu also extended the philosophical concepts of "hsing" (forms) and "ming" (names). "Hsing" referred to the duties of an official. "Ming" referred to the performance of the official. And "ming" had to match "hsing". An official would be rewarded only when his performance matched what he was expected to do at a given position; he would be punished if he had done more than or less than what he should have. Strict matching of duties and performance had to be adhered to. No subordinate should overstep his own position, and performance was assessed strictly against the call of duty. To a large degree, ideas underlying these concepts are still applicable to the management of a modern organization. Some examples are:

* Clearly-delineated status structure
* Concentration of power at the top
* Numerous and specific administrative procedures, rules, and regulations - formal and written
* Clearly-defined duties and responsibilities
* Task specialization
* Evaluation of employees by performance and merit
* Motivation of employees by both rewards and punishments

To sum up, in contrast to Confucianism that advocated autonomy, Legalism emphasized strict rule and control in order to maintain law and order in a hierarchic society.

THE GREAT MANAGER OF ANCIENT CHINA

In the year 221 BC, Ch'in Shihuang - "The First Emperor" - founded the dynasty that unified the country and gave China its present name in Western languages. The discovery of the 2,200-year-old terracotta army on a grand scale in 1974 at his imperial tomb has not only attracted a big crowd of tourists but also provided invaluable materials for understanding the long history of Chinese politics, technology, and society. Emperor Ch'in Shihuang's work, as recorded in history books and left behind in ancient remains, also indicates that the First Emperor of China was indeed the Great Manager by any standards.

Today, the functions of managers are generally classified into planning, organizing, staffing, directing, and controlling. Planning involves selecting the course of action that an enterprise will follow. Organizing involves establishing an intentional structure of roles for people in an enterprise to fill. Staffing involves filling, and keeping filled, the positions provided for by organization structure. Directing is influencing people so that they will strive willingly and enthusiastically toward the achievement of organization and group goals. Controlling is the measurement and correction of subordinates' activities to assure that outcomes conform to plans. Let us now examine briefly how the Great Manager of ancient time performed each one of these functions.

After unifying the country, the Emperor had made several important decisions, which subsequently left strong imprints on the development of China as a nation. For example, he decided to standardize ancient China's laws, currency, roads, weights and measures, axle lengths, and written language. He also decided to embark on vast and complex construction projects. Looking today at the outcomes of these decisions, as most vividly manifested in such major projects as the building of the Great Wall and the Imperial Tomb near modern Xian in north central China, Ch'in Shihuang could certainly be regarded as a planner of exceptional vision and capability.

The Emperor established the centralized government and ran the empire by dividing it into 36 commanderies, which in turn were subdivided into districts or prefectures. Each commandery was under the authority of a civil administrator and a military governor. Appointed by and responsible to the central government, these two top officials worked under the watchful eye of an overseer. This centralized bureaucratic organization left no room for feudalism and, in a modified form, it was to be the basis of the imperial system in China down to the turn of this century. To fill and keep filled the positions thus provided for, the Emperor made use of talents, gathering around him the able staff and only promoting the meritorious, regardless of their original backgrounds. Prime Minister Li Hsu, his chief adviser, was not even a native of Ch'in; and the renowned water engineer, Cheng Kuo, who contributed greatly to the state by overseeing the digging of a major drainage and irrigation scheme, first came as a spy to the capital of Ch'in [3].

In order to direct the people toward the achievement of his empire's goals, the Emperor adopted the doctrine which was based on a belief in strict law and order, i.e. Legalism. He did not hesitate to use severe punishments to deal with the opposition, burning books and burying scholars alive [4]. As for control, the Emperor attended to matters personally and undertook frequent tours of the empire. It is said that he was well informed about the affairs of state, each day reading piles of reports and documents, and would not rest until he had finished with them. Having examined the way he had performed the planning, organizing, staffing, directing, and controlling functions, we could conclude that Ch'in Shihuang was indeed an exceptionally effective manager. Without any doubt, he had laid down a solid foundation for the formation of China's management tradition.

GLIMPSE OF MANAGEMENT PRACTICES TODAY

In a still rather closed society like China, where a mixed economy (i.e. a combination of socialistic and capitalistic economies) is at present being experimented, it is extremely difficult to find out exactly what the practices of management are like. However, a small collection of the following cases, gathered over the past five years on my visits to China, might be useful for getting at least a glimpse of the practices.

Case 1: Travel Bureau

Owing to the language barrier as well as numerous bureaucratic red-tapes imposed on travellers, the great majority of tourists from abroad have no choice but to rely on the state-run travel bureau, which offers services ranging from securing visas and bookings with airlines and hotels down to determining where and what to eat in China. This is necessary in spite of hefty fees charged by the bureau, whose offices are found today in most major cities inside and outside China. One naturally expects that the packaged tour arranged by the bureau will go smoothly without a hitch from the start to the end. Yet, as more and more Chinese cities and towns are opened to foreign tourists, an increasing number of complaints are being heard about the low quality of services actually rendered once in China - e.g. an unscheduled sleepover at the waiting-room of a remote airport due to the last minute flight cancellation, an on-the-spot change to the originally agreed-upon itinerary due to overbooking at a hotel, a sudden switch from airplane to train due to booking error and so on.
    Not so long ago, my own self-arranged adventure in China turned into a nightmare. Given a warning that the booking of China's domestic flights must be made at least one week beforehand, I visited the bureau's branch office in City A to book a flight from City B (my next stop) to City C (the final destination). The conversation that took place between a travel agent (A) and myself (M) went something like this:

M - "Are there any flights from City B to City C next Monday, that is exactly one week from today?"

A - "Yes, I think so."

M - "Oh, good! I would like to buy a ticket for an afternoon flight on that day."

A - "Sorry, I cannot sell you the ticket."

M - "Why not? There are still some seats available, aren't there?"

A - "I would suppose so, but you cannot buy the ticket here."

M - " ....."

A - "Since you will be taking off from City B, you can only buy the ticket from our City B branch."

M - "That's amazing. Could you then at least give them a call to book a seat for me, please?"

A - "It is not our policy to take a reservation over the phone. You must go there first, OK?"

M - "But, ..."

I could not get any further with this agent, who appeared more anxious to get rid of me than to offer much-needed help. Four days later, immediately upon reaching City B, I rushed over to the bureau's branch office. But this visit again turned out to be equally futile and frustrating; "Sorry, all flights to City C are now booked solid for the next five days", was the only answer I could get. At the end, I somehow managed to buy a ticket at the local railway station for an uncomfortable 3-day trip to my final destination. In most industrialized countries, the management of information resources has become as important as that of all other resources of an enterprise. However, what I had experienced during this trip was a series of unnecessary frustrations largely caused by communication problems within the travel bureau. One of the important functions of management, particularly in organizing, is a provision for coordination of activities, authority, and information horizontally and vertically in an organization. This case reveals a lack of such provision, resulting in failure to assign tasks, necessary to accomplish goals, to people lower down the organizational hierarchy.

Case 2: Hotel

I once stayed in a rather somber-looking 450-room hotel, built in 1962, in the capital city of China's northwestern province. Its main restaurant is widely acclaimed as the place to taste some of the region's speciality dishes. Yet I was totally dismayed by the turtle-slow services provided by its staff. The hotel guests were often seen unattended at tables with dirty dishes left behind by the diners before them; some even chose to clear up the table themselves when all the efforts to get attention had been ignored by the restaurant's staff, who seemed to be conveniently looking the other way. To make things worse, there appeared to be no manager or supervisor in sight who could easily be identified as the person in charge.

After staying in the hotel for nearly a week, I got acquainted well enough with one of the more friendly female staff to pose a burning question: "Why, on earth, are you all waiting on us so slowly?" Her response was most revealing, and I soon started seeing at least the tip of underlying problems. Basically, major gripes that she and other staff held about their job were, in her own words:

"I don't particularly like the job itself."
After graduating from a local secondary school, she took a state-administered examination for job assignment; and the restaurant job she got at the end was not what she had really wanted herself (i.e. foreign tourist guide or interpreter). Naturally, like most other staff in the restaurant, she is not happy with the job, and feels that her own personal development through the job is very limited.

"I resent the long working hours."
She works 9 hours serving 3 meals a day, and gets one day off every 5 days. Though this sounds quite reasonable, the actual working hours stretch from 6:30 a.m. in the morning to 9:30 p.m. in the evening. The restaurant staff are all provided with a bed in the dormitory at the hotel to take rest between meals and, if they wish, to sleep overnight. This seemingly comfortable and considerate arrangement was, in reality, not received

very favorably by young workers mostly in their late teens and early twenties.

"The hotel management even refuses to accept the fact that problems actually exist."
This complaint was rather odd in view of the fact that Guest Opinion Cards were placed on every table for the diners to rate the services provided at the restaurant. I soon learned that most guests stayed at the hotel only one or two nights and normally did not bother to fill in the card. This lack of feedback from the guests was interpreted by the hotel management as an indication of satisfactory services. The female staff lamented, "The management does neither understand our need for personal development nor recognize the deeply-rooted resentment over the existing work arrangements. By purposely working slowly and offering only mediocre services, we are really hoping that more guests will file their complaints and put pressure on our management."

This case points out problems related, in large part, to three functions of management, namely:

Staffing   – This includes inventory, appraisal and selection of staff for positions; compensating; and training or otherwise developing current job holders.

Directing   – This has to do with the mostly interpersonal aspect of management, which deals with problems arising from people, their desires and attitudes, and their behavior as individuals and in groups.

Controlling – This measures performance against goals and objectives, shows where negative deviations exist, and, by putting in motion actions to correct deviations, helps ensure the accomplishment of goals and objectives.

Case 3: Factory

While on a seminar trip to a thriving industrial city in central China, I had received a visit from an engineer working at a pipe fabricating factory with over 15,000 workers. A few years ago, as a part of its drive toward modernization, the factory management decided to automate the entire fabricating process through the use of a computer-based process control system. After their initial plan to purchase a turn-key system from a major US computer manufacturer fell through, largely due to their unique and stringent requirements, each of the five departments involved in the fabricating process was authorized to go ahead and purchase a process controller separately. The outspoken engineer, who had just been appointed to the project coordinator, confessed: "We are in a big mess. We designed an automated process control system, which appeared to work very nicely on paper, and then allowed each department to select and order its own equipment without much mutual consultation and thought given to interface problems." He continued, "We now have at hand a central control processor as well, which is supposed to coordinate the work of all these individual equipments. Yet nobody knows how to make it work."

Trapped in such an impossible situation, he should perhaps start looking for a job elsewhere. However, in the society where the rejection of jobs assigned by the state-authority could easily lead to a less desirable assignment or even unemployment, it is easier said than done. This case illustrates a total lack of well-thought planning on the part of the factory management. Planning is deciding in advance what to do, how to do, when to do, and who is to do. It implies not only the introduction of new things but also sensible and workable innovation. Having failed to follow this very basic principle of management, it is not surprising at all that the ambitious work to automate the factory came to a grinding halt.

Case 4: Research Institute

When I first visited the institute in the late 1970s, its computer center was equipped with an outdated second-generation computer and a couple of microcomputers. Today, supported by the central government's new program for modernization in science and technology, it boasts the installation of a modern fourth-generation computer as well as nearly twenty personal computers of various makes and models. Personal computers are being used mainly to develop computerized Management Information Systems (MIS), but the actual fruit of their efforts to date in this area appears to be minimal. The Deputy Director of the institute admitted:

> "We are very short of qualified staff, particularly in the commercial application area. That lady over there, for example, must look after the development of new application software as well as the maintenance of the hardware and systems software. Her section has already computerized the payroll and several other basic accounting systems, but they still have a long way to go before integrating all these and proposed application systems now in the pipeline into a total MIS."

With a short supply of well-trained staff and no formal maintenance contract signed with any foreign computer manufacturers, this overworked section head is forced to spend a good part of her working day solving numerous operations and maintenance problems herself only with the aid of vendor-supplied manuals, all written in English. Due to an acute shortage of talents, a clear assignment of organizational activities and delegation of authority, though recognized as absolutely necessary by the management, seem to be still far from realization. In order to alleviate the problem, the institute has, in recent years, sent abroad several senior researchers, including the Deputy Director. Some of them have already returned to work after two years of further study in computer technology as well as management. Perhaps this is, unlike the organizations described in the three other cases, why they seem to be at least more aware of the existing managerial problems. Looking at the way in which the management has upgraded the main computer system, has reorganized the organizational structure, has trained and developed the staff, has boosted the staff morale by offering better working conditions, and has transferred out some redundant staff based on performance appraisal, we could say that their efforts are at least being directed in the right direction toward the installation of a more efficient and effective management system.

BRAVE NEW EXPERIMENTS

All four cases above illustrate various problems associated with the management. The first two are of service organizations. Here, we are struck with an impression that such a modern marketing concept as "Consumers are the King" is almost totally missing. The absence of the concept may be explained, to a considerable degree, by the external environment that surrounds these organizations, which is obviously quite different from that of other developed nations in the West. For one thing, the current economic system, that offers little incentive to individuals, could well explain why the hotel and travel bureau staff behave the way they do; the technological and educational factors that prevail in China today would also provide some explanations for the existence of problems facing the factory and the research institute.

Alternatively, they could be explained by China's political system, that often puts ideological soundness ahead of professional competence in job allocation by the state. Contrasts between the doctrines of Confucianism and Legalism have already been described. The contrasts are not a mere matter of ancient history. They are vididly alive in the most recent history of Chinese politics. Since the Communists gained power in 1949, government policy has always been changing, like a pendulum swinging from left to right and back again. For example, the Cultural Revolution (1967-1976) was a swing to the left. When it went too far, it simply had to swing back to the right. Whereas late Chairman Mao Zedong, who often compared himself to Emperor Ch'in Shihuang, had followed the doctrine of Legalism, the current political leader Deng Xiaoping has adopted more of the

Confucian doctrine and given more automomy to local governments and enterprises.

Since the latest shakeup in China's political leadership in the late 1970s, serious efforts have been made to reform its economic, management, and education systems. Economic reforms, that had begun in 1978 to carry out the country's ambitious modernization program, seem to be making some progress but have also created serious problems. The problems mainly concern corruption, individual incomes, high prices, and work postings [5]. The corruption and scandals have increased over the past few years along with economic reforms. Perhaps the best-publicized one is the "Hainan Scandal", that led to an abrupt awakening for the Chinese leadership on the pitfalls of fast economic development through short cuts. On Hainan island - China's second largest island next to Taiwan, free-trade zone and open-port in the Gulf of Tonkin - local party officials misused the economic automomy and converted local funds into more than US$1.6 billion on the black market. They then used the money to import 89,000 cars, 122,000 motorcycles, 2.8 million television sets, and 252,000 video recorders, which they promptly resold throughout China at two and three times the original cost [6].

Popular dissatisfaction with the wide gap between individual incomes stems from the government's attempts to put an end to 30 years of "eating out of the same pot" mental state - a rather well-established egalitarian idea under Chairman Mao Zedong. The reform, aiming at linking income to production, has often been bogged down by this long-accustomed idea and bureaucratic inertia. According to the surveys conducted recently by the government, the Chinese appear to be more concerned about their incomes than rising prices. The fourth problem concerns the arbitrary work postings through the state job allocation plan. In fact, the resentment over the non-circulation of the labor force has long been a major grievance, particularly among China's young generation.

Although the attitude and behavior of people at work are necessarily influenced by the environment surrounding an organization, they are no doubt more directly affected by the management. The selected cases above, in fact, highlight the problems of different kinds and degrees, which are closely related to the process of management. As a means to solve these problems, Chinese authorities recently announced a move to expand and strengthen the responsibility system for state-run enterprises [7]. This system aims at making factory directors at half of the country's 54,000 state-run enterprises in 22 provinces fully responsible for management decisions - including hiring and firing - by the end of 1987. Special offices have already been set up all over the country to ensure that party officials adhere to the system, which was first introduced as an experiment back in 1984.

More recently, the State Economic Commission decided to conduct a study on the performance of large state enterprises, many of which had reported losses [8]. This move is seen as part of China's economic reforms which seek to breathe new life into stagnant enterprises by making them shoulder their own profit and loss accounts. It is believed that the performance of the enterprises will be measured against product quality, the standard of technology used, consumption level of raw materials and energy, productivity, the return on investment, profits, and the workers' per capita tax paid to the state. This is in marked contrast to the previous practice which used the gross value of industrial output as the sole criterion. One option being considered by the Economic Commission is to provide better performing enterprises with more automony to give bonuses to their workers as an incentive.

Management is not merely a process but also a philosophy. The philosophy may be broadly defined in terms of the attitudes of an organization toward its external and internal agents, i.e. the implied and expressed attitudes toward employees, consumers, suppliers, government, and society. Since the end of the Cultural Revolution in 1976, China, as a nation, has gone through several significant changes in her attitudes toward external agents, particuarly toward foreigners. Major changes include:

* Foreign investment is not an economic infiltration but a contributor to increased financial strength and technology transfer.

* Foreign trade should not be discouraged for the sake of self-sufficiency but needs to be encouraged to earn more foreign currencies.
* Permitting foreign involvement in resource extraction is not a traitor's act but a necessity to enable China's national development.
* Tourism is not just a way to cultivate friendship but also a means to earn foreign currencies.

As clearly reflected in these attitudinal changes, China has indeed opened her once tightly closed society to the outside world to formulate the new philosophy of management, carefully adapting the models imported from abroad to its own needs. The philosophy will then have to be learned and accepted by a majority of people before it can be successfully applied to the actual practice of management. Yet, to many Chinese, management is still a little-known concept that needs to be understood before anything else can be done. In fact, the government of China today believes that education holds the key to the on-going management reforms. Only four days after the top leader Deng Xiaoping announced his wish to step down from his most important post on the Politburo Standing Committee - the party's supreme decision making body - at the 13th Chinese Communist Party Congress to be held in October 1987, a Communist Party weekly said, "The task is to choose and prepare thousands of young people for leading positions at all levels ... Potential leaders and officials should be young, professionally competent, ideologically sound, and in good health" [9]. It is significant that ideological soundness is placed third behind youthfulness and professional competence as the qualities required to become China's future leaders. Since the adoption of the party's Central Committee resolution on sweeping changes in education, several important measures have already been implemented to turn the aims into reality. These include a bigger national budget for education (up 11 per cent in 1985 compared with the previous year), setting up an education board above ministry level to eliminate all obstacles to educational reform, and intensifying general as well as special and vocational education [10].

Many of the nation's 1.1 billion people lost out on education during the 10-year-long Cultural Revolution. Education then was given little emphasis, and the sluggish economy provided little incentive for young people to study. To remedy the situation, China's current efforts for educational reforms are being waged on all fronts. Some 1.1 million students, enrolled in fast-expanding vocational education, are taking courses in medium level management and technology. And an increasing number of China's over 1,000 universities and colleges have formally introduced high-level management courses. For example, right across the border from Hong Kong, in Shenzhen - one of the four Special Economic Zones where the country's brave experiments in mixed economy are making a headway - a brand-new university was established to run, among others, an American-style MBA program. Shenzhen University, a strong advocate for dimisnishing the involvement of the state authorities in university affairs, has just dismantled the state job allocation plan to allow its students to compete with each other for employment [11]. Students graduating from the university in 1987 were to present their grades, a resume of their extracurricular activities, and a two-minute video presentation to prospective employers. More than half the class of 1987 had already signed contracts with the employers. This experiment being carried out in Shenzhen and at an elite handful of China's universities and colleges aims to alleviate students resentment over the non-circulation of the labor force.

Besides the expansion of management courses, academic exchange programs of all kinds have also been set up with numerous universities in Hong Kong and abroad. And tens of thousands of scholars and students have been sent out for further study in order to learn the latest developments in management and other technologies. However, a recent statement made by a senior education official in Beijing points to the surfacing of serious concern about the effectiveness of such exchange programs. The statement read: "Government-sponsored students, under Chinese regulations, should return to the country." [12] It appears to be a stern warning to Chinese students, some of whom have sought to remain abroad after the completion of their studies. Since 1978, China has sent out more than 28,000 students and scholars to the US, but only about 8,000 have returned to China. Those who have already returned complain that they cannot use their skills and knowledge that they have learned overseas.

CATCHING UP ON LOST TIME

We need to remind ourselves that China represents one of the world's oldest civilizations and its ancient city of Xian (the capital established in 221 BC by Emperor Ch'in Shihuan) was the starting point of the famed Silk Road, along which the traders of ancient time took with them not only the much-prized goods but also the far-advanced knowledge that China then had to offer to the rest of the world. In fact, China had one of the greatest managers of all times in the person of Emperor Ch'in Shihuang, who had ruled the vast empire through the effective use of centralized bureaucracy more than 2,200 years ago.

Following the open door policy, introduced only a decade ago, the Chinese turned to the West for help in the areas of management education and training. However, they have also begun to show an active interest in their own management tradition through the readings of the classics. "Art of War" has emerged as a favorite, and today there are several publications in China that attempt to relate this classic to managerial thinking and practice [13]. It was written at about the time of Ch'in Shihuang's reign by China's well-known military strategist Sun Tzu, whose thoughts had been much influenced by the earlier doctrines of Confucianism and Legalism. Sun Tzu highlighted five virtues that a military leader must have. They were: "chih" (wisdom), "hsin" (faithfulness), "jen" (benevolent love), "yong" (courage), and "yan" (discipline). By "chih", he meant the ability to recognize changing circumstances and to act expediently. "Hsin" referred to the ability to gain complete trust from subordinates, and "jen" humanity and the ability to sympathize with others. "Yong" meant bravery and decisiveness, and "yan" the ability to command respect and rule strictly and fairly. It is interesting to note that the first three are exactly same as the Confucian virtues, whereas the last one is that emphasized by the Legalists.

Sun Tzu also advocated seven strategic factors that would form the prerequisites for warfare. In fact, as shown in Table A-1, they hold important implications for the management of modern business organizations as well [14]. In essence, the first two listed in the table represent the external factors, while all others are the internal factors of the organization; the third and fourth factors (i.e. strengths, doctrine or law) mainly deal with the organization, and the following three more directly with the management. Taken together, these strategies for winning a war, advocated by Sun Tzu, are very comprehensive in scope and coverage. They are, in fact, very relevant for applications to management today. Given such comprehensiveness, one could perhaps contend that the framework for corporate strategy, as we understand today, had already been laid out in China some 2,200 years ago.

Ancient China's great philosophers such as Confucius and Han Fei Tzu had also taught the rulers of their time moral principles, many of which are still applicable to the management of modern organizations. It is true that modern management is largely of Western origin; but, the theories of management were developed in the West only at the turn of this century. Perhaps we must give more credit to the Chinese for having developed the principles of management long before management took a root in the West as an independent academic discipline. The world has gone through many changes since; and today China, after decades of stagnation, is the country that is in dire need of management reforms. China's current bid to breathe new life into its economy could be seen as an effort to catch up on lost time and to restore its time-honored tradition in management.

Table A-1: Sun Tzu's Seven Strategic Factors for Warfare

Moral Influence	Political leadership within the country. The government must provide leadership to business in the form of proper legal system as well as effective directives and policies.
Weather and Terrain	Environmental factors of the company. The company must adapt to changes in its primary and secondary environments.
Strengths	Competitive edge of the company. The company must acquire sufficient resources such as manpower, materials, money, equipment, and technologies, from its surrounding environment in order to gain relative strengths.
Doctrine or Law	Organizational structure of the company. The company must be organized in such a way that policies, procedures, rules, and regulations are effectively executed through the proper channels of communication and along the clearly-defined lines of authority and responsibility.
Command	Corporated leadership in the company. The management must lead employees based on the 5 virtues of wisdom, faithfulness, benevolent love, courage, and discipline.
Training	Human resource development. The management must recognize the particular importance of manpower as an expandable organizational resource, and must therefore train employees in order to gain greater competitive edge.
Discipline	Comprehensive disciplinary system. The management must motivate employees by both rewards and punishments.

NOTES

1. Fairbank, J.K., <u>The United States and China</u>, Cambridge, MA: Harvard University Press, (1979), p.59

2. Tan, C.H., "The Management of Thoughts of Han Fei Tzu", <u>Proceedings of the Academy of International Business (Southeast Asia region) Conference</u> (1986), pp.2-21

3. Cotterell, A., <u>The First Emperor of China</u>, London: Papermac, (1981)

4. Clayre, C., <u>The Heart of the Dragon</u>, Glasgow: William Collins Sons & Co., (1984)

5. <u>South China Morning Post</u>, "China Focus: Reforms Fail to Please All", (Jun. 8, 1987), p.20

6. <u>Newsweek</u>, "Caught Speeding on the Capitalist Road", (Aug. 15, 1985), p.37

7. <u>South China Morning Post</u>, "China Focus: Manger Control System to Grow", (Jun. 8, 1987) p.20

8. <u>Business Post</u> (South China Morning Post, Jun. 16, 1987), "China Bid to Breathe New Life into State Firms", p.1

9. <u>South China Morning Post</u>, "China: Official Call for Younger Leaders", (Jun. 9, 1987), p.9

10. <u>South China Morning Post</u>, "Big Push to Let the Lost Generation Catch Up", (Aug. 19, 1985) p.10

11. <u>South China Morning Post</u>, "China: Students Test the Open Job Market", (Jun. 9, 1987) p.9

12. <u>South China Morning Post</u>, "China: Young Chinese Studying Overseas Must Return", (Jun. 6, 1987), p.5

13. Li, S.J., X.J. Yang and J.R. Tang, <u>Sun Tzu's Art of War and Business Management</u>, People's Republic of China: Kwansi People's Press, (1984); National Economic Commission, <u>Classical Chinese Thoughts and Modern Management</u>, People's Republic of China: Yunnan People's Publication, (1985)

14. Wee, C.H., "Sun Tzu's Art of War: Prerequisites for Strategic Planning", <u>Proceedings of the Academy of International Business (Southeast Asia region) Conference</u>, (1986), pp.22-30

Adler, N.J. (1986), <u>International Dimension of Organization Behavior</u>, Boston: Kent Publishing Co.

Burks, A.W. (1981), <u>Japan: Profile of a Postindustrial Power</u>, Boulder, Colorado: Westview Press

Clark, R. (1979), <u>The Japanese Company</u>, New Haven: Yale University Press

Clegg, S.R., D.C. Dunphy and S.G. Redding (1986), <u>The Enterprise and Management in East Asia</u>, Hong Kong: Center of Asian Studies

Drucker, P.F. (1954), <u>The Practice of Management</u>, New York: Harper & Row

England, G.W. (1975), <u>The Manager and His Values: An International Perspective from the United States, Japan, Korea, India and Australia</u>, Cambridge, MA: Ballinger

Haire, M., E.E. Ghiselli and L.W. Porter (1966), <u>Managerial Thinking: An International Study</u>, New York: John Wiley & Sons

Hertzberg, F. (1966), <u>Work and the Nature of Man</u>, Cleveland, OH: The World Publishing Co.

Hofstede, G. (1984), <u>Culture's Consequences: International Differences in Work-related Values</u>, Beverly Hills, CA: Sage Publications

Iwata, R. (1982), <u>Japanese-style Management</u>, Tokyo: Asian Productivity Organization

Kahn, H. (1979), <u>World Economic Development: 1979 and Beyond</u>, London: Croom Helm

Masatsugu, M. (1985), <u>Management and Society- Lessons from Contemporary Japan</u>, Singapore: Federal Publications

Mintzberg, H. (1980), <u>The Nature of Managerial Work</u>, Englewood Cliffs: Prentice-Hall

Morita, A. (1987), <u>Made in Japan</u>, London: Collins

Nakane, C. (1970), <u>Japanese Society</u>, London: Weidenfeld & Nicolson

Ouchi, W.G. (1981), <u>Theory Z : How American Business can meet the Japanese Challenges</u>, New York: Avon Books

Pascale, R.T. and A.G. Athos (1981), <u>The Art of Japanese Management: Applications for American Executives</u>, New York: Simon & Schuster

Peters, T.J. and R.H. Waterman (1982), <u>In Search of Excellence: Lessons from America's Best-run Companies</u>, New York: Harper & Row

Reischauer, E.O. (1977), <u>The Japanese</u>, Tokyo: Charles E. Tuttle

Sethi, S.P., N. Namiki and C.L. Swanson (1984), <u>The False Promise of Japanese Miracle</u>, London: Pitman

Silin, R.H. (1976), <u>Leadership and Values: The Organization of Large-scale Taiwanese Enterprises</u>, Cambridge, MA: Harvard University Press

Vogel, E.F. (1979), <u>Japan as Number One: Lessons for America</u>, Cambridge, MA: Harvard University Press

Vroom, V.H. (1964), <u>Work and Motivation</u>, New York: John Wiley & Sons

Yoshino, M.Y. (1968), <u>Japan's Managerial System: Tradition and Innovation</u>, Cambridge, MA: MIT Press